Thank God for Prayer

By Russell W. Lake

Unity Books
Unity Village, Missouri

Cover design by Jeri Robinson

Contents

Why Pray?

Consider these facts:

—About 150 million persons in the United States are members of a church or religious organization.

—94 percent of all Americans, in a poll, have declared that they believe in God or a universal spirit.

—54 percent, in the same poll, said their religion is very important to them.

Consider these questions:

—How many of the 150 million pray?

—What percent of the Americans who believe get answers to their prayers?

—Is it possible for prayer not to be answered?

Would you believe that *everyone* prays, all the time, in one way or another? And make no mistake: every prayer is answered. This Truth is absolute, undeniable. But it can be discouraging to us to pray earnestly, yet again and again fail to experience *desired* results. We pray for health, and perhaps continue to suffer sickness; for peace, and discord remains; and for prosperity, and we still lack the money to meet our needs. We learn that the act of praying, no matter how assiduously exercised, does not invariably guarantee fulfillment.

A Potent Force

On the other hand, it is demonstrably true that prayer is far and away the most potent force we can call upon in the universe. Can atomic fusion or fission on a grand scale perform the miracle of healing? Can the explosion of a hydrogen bomb produce prosperity where lack exists? Can it transform bitter discord into serene harmony, or eliminate injustice from any situation? Prayer can, and does. Tennyson said: *More things are wrought by prayer than this world dreams of.*

If prayer is that powerful, that effectual, why do our prayers consistently seem to fail to produce, to make things happen? The apostle James wrote: *You ask and do not receive, because you ask wrongly....* (James 4:3)

Why do we continue to pray when, regardless of resolute perseverance in prayer, we still experience failure to manifest our desires? Is it because of habit, or because of a lingering hope that somehow, someday, God may get around to granting our desires? Is it perhaps because we are afraid of being punished if we do not pray? Or is it because of a deep-seated genetic force that impels us to pray and keep on praying? People have always prayed. It was the French philosopher Voltaire who first said: *If God did not exist it would be necessary to invent him.* The history of mankind is replete with evidence that every race in every age has had its gods or god to fear, to love, to propitiate, to offer sacrifices to, to abase themselves before, or to call upon for help. Paleontologists and archaeologists have long known that people in the dim mists of antiquity stood in awe of primitive gods and practiced elaborate rituals to ensure that they remained in the good graces of all the super-beings and super-forces.

Since people first began to think, to fear, to

desire, to doubt their self-sufficiency, they have prayed, and they are still praying. At first they prayed to many gods—gods of war, of peace, of destruction, floods, and winds; gods of fertility, life, and death. Religions were founded on superstitions and fear, fear of a God of judgment. With our present-day concepts, we would consider a religion that called for live animal offerings or human sacrifices as very primitive. Such a God is a long way from a God of love and forgiveness as we know Him to be.

One God

As civilization advanced, the majority of people settled on one God, one all-powerful God, to be the embodiment of all former gods. They prayed to Him to solve their problems and to satisfy their needs.

Even so, the single God took many forms. Even today, in what we consider an enlightened age, there exist diametrically opposed concepts of Him. Some still see Him as an angry deity, thundering dictums from His throne in heaven, visiting the punishment of hell upon transgressors, and rewarding those who obey Him. Others feel His presence as

benign, an omnipresent Spirit in whose benef-
icence toward all His sons and daughters
there is no judgment, no punishment, only
love. But God is not a jealous God. He does
not judge us by what we call Him. He hears
all prayers. We need only to *experience* Him
to receive His gifts.

But with all the opposing notions of the
form of God, must we first come to agree on
His true form before we can successfully pray
to Him? If this were true, it would mean that
one creed has sole access to Him and all
others pray in vain. This is not true. Prayers
are answered in every language, whether He
is called God, Allah, Krishna, the sun, the
Man Upstairs, or Spirit.

Pray to the God of your heart, and He will
reveal Himself to you as your personal God,
the Lord of your being. Pray to Him in
perfect faith, and your prayers will be
answered. You do not feel it necessary to
pray that at midnight tonight a new day will
begin. In the same degree of positive knowing, make your desires known to God.

In Unity we see God as omnipresent, omnipotent Spirit. Some of us may insist that
ours is the true concept, but we do not deny
others the privilege of worshiping Him

according to their own concepts. God is the Supreme Being in whatever form we may image Him. The form is less important than that we *feel* His Presence, *know* His love, and *express* unswerving faith in Him.

Even if you are confused by the many religious beliefs and do not have a clear concept of God, do not hesitate to pray. Hold fast to the image of the thing you want to have manifested, believe you have received it, and you will be praying to God. He will answer your prayer of faith. The apostle James wrote: *. . . and the prayer of faith will save the sick man . . . .* (James 5:15)

Our impulse to pray, our continuing *need* to pray, is an ingrained part of our being in the same way that love of family is a part of us, or self-preservation is an inescapable ingredient of our nature. It is the natural thing to do. So why not learn to make prayer work?

Prayer, which is basically a simple and straightforward communion with God, has been modified by dogmas of religious orders down through the ages until it has become, to many, an esoteric and mysterious procedure beyond the understanding of the uninitiated. Some appear to believe that truly effectual prayer comes only through those with special training, or through those especially anointed.

All Are Equal

Yet we know intuitively that all are equal in the sight of God. We are not lesser creatures. This is confirmed by no less an authority than Jesus Christ, who assured us it is true. Education, position, even special training do not give anyone preferred status. The only requirement for effectual prayer is understanding—understanding the forces of prayer, and understanding our relationship with God. All else follows.

Prayer is not an involved process, nor is it mysterious. It is not a formalized ritual of repetitive gestures or incantations. It does not require a go-between to intercede with the higher power. Prayer is directly to the God of your being within and about you, everywhere present.

Charles Fillmore defined prayer as a communion between man and God. This is prayer in the ideal, to which we should aspire. Many books have been written about how to attain this pure state of communion. We do not really need to be taught formalized rules of prayer. We need only to realize how we fit into the structure of being, and we will then know that we can talk with Him as we would with a loving Father who holds in trust for us the fulfillment of every desire that evolves within us.

Although prayer in essence is simple to define, even to practice, we build ramifications that carry it beyond our comprehension. Since the beginning of consciousness, few persons have perceived the full power of prayer, or even its true purpose. Jesus Christ was one who did. Others, seeing the great works wrought by prayer, have milled outside the wall clamoring to be allowed the knowledge of how to pray.

We witness a miracle of healing through prayer in a great tabernacle or a hospital or simple home, and our curiosity demands to know how it was done. We seek and find no answers because no one knows. People tell us of forms and rituals, but they cannot tell us how prayer works, or why. We are faced with indisputable proof that prayer does work, and in that confidence we pray without formal instruction but earnestly seeking an answer to a need. Suddenly we become aware that our prayer is answered, but we cannot explain how it came about. Enthusiastically we continue to pray, fired by success. Our prayers continue to be fulfilled. But we have failures too, and we wonder why. At last the realization steals upon us that the prayers that accomplish their missions are those we believe in. We remember that prayers that *seemed* to be unanswered raised gnawing doubts in our minds in the beginning. At last we become aware that our prayers are answered when our consciousness accepts the answer.

There is in all of us an intuitive knowing that life is beautiful. Happiness and fulfillment are ours by divine right, embodied in the perfection of our creation. God created no imperfect beings. He ordained no failures, no unsound bodies, no fearing minds, no deficient lives.

Divine Perfection

This is not to say that when one manifests something other than perfection in mind and body, according to our interpretation of perfection, he is subject to blame. Nor can those associated with him, peers or forebears, be judged. None among us in our abysmal ignorance of the interplay of forces in the inner or outer universe knows all the causes, all the effects. This we know: God does not decree affliction upon any of His beloved children. By His very nature, He cannot. God sees only good, works only good; this we have learned. A seeming malformation in our makeup may be a blessing to us and to others. Perhaps the blessing could come in no other way. No one is ever outside the circle of God, beyond the love and care of God. Our souls choose the means of their unfoldment.

When we experience adversity, we know intuitively that we have gone astray. Scarcely anyone believes that God intended life to be permanently thorny and unmanageable. When we are sick or poor or unhappy, we naturally seek change. Divine order is the law of the universe, and when we seem out of order, we tend to rebel. Some misguided persons may think that God is punishing them for a transgression; others feel that God has turned His back on them, leaving them to fend for themselves. Some accept the falsehood that evil is a substantive entity in the world which, through its devious machinations, has triumphed. Others accept the truth that they simply have gotten off the track.

Rebellion takes many forms. It can be good or bad. To those who believe adversity is a temporary misfortune brought on by failure to think and act in accordance with the law of God, rebellion can be good, because through it they are impelled to seek corrective measures. To those who feel God is responsible, either as an act of punishment or through failure to help, rebellion can be bad. It may take the form of bitterness or hopelessness which, by its inevitable effect of separation in mind from God, pushes the restoration further away. To those who believe their afflictions are brought upon them by another person or group of persons, or by life itself, rebellion is particularly bad because it often results in hatred or even violence. Bitterness, hopelessness, and hatred are aberrant forms of prayer, unknowing in their application but with boomerang effects.

Praying Aright

Everyone prays in some way. Those who open their minds and hearts to the truth of God pray aright.

What constitutes prayer? Is it affirmation? Is it denial of error? Is it meditation? Is it making one's desires known and listening for God's response? Is it simply having faith in God to right all wrongs? It is all these and much more.

When we come to know what prayer is, we also arrive at an agreement of what prayer is not. It is not supplication; nor is it begging or imploring; it is not self-abasement; it is not selfish demanding; it is not anxious importuning for help; it is not a request that one's enemies be brought to grief.

The nineteenth century poet James Montgomery wrote: *Prayer is the soul's sincere desire, uttered or unexpressed . . . .* It is the soul's sincere desire to bring forth the good that we intuitively know has belonged to us from the beginning. This means that our prayers are affirmations of good. They ring with confidence and never waver in fear. According to Mark, Jesus said: *"Therefore I tell you, whatever you ask in prayer, believe that you have received it, and it will be yours."* (Mark 11:24) Prayer is not confronting God and insisting that He pay attention to us and our complaints. It is not even reminding Him of some good that we are in need of and asking that He bestir Himself and get it for us. Matthew also reported that

Jesus said: "*. . . for your Father knows what you need before you ask him.*" (Matt. 6:8)

If God knows what we need before we ask, why do we pray? Furthermore, why hasn't He fulfilled our need?

We Cannot Change Him

We must realize that our prayers do not change God. It is fortunate that we cannot change Him. Can you imagine the chaos in our lives if, in our immaturity and incomplete concepts, we could twist Omnipotence to our will? God knows our needs. He desires to fulfill them. Our prayers are to open the gates of our minds, constricted by fears and impatience, to let His good flow in. This takes faith—faith in the possibility of our desires, faith in God's ability to provide them, faith in our worthiness to receive. Jesus said you must believe you have received before you can have your wish, and in this there is no thought of changing God but of changing you, changing your mind from unbelief to total faith. The successful prayer is the prayer of faith.

Pray and expect your prayer to be answered. You will need to rid yourself of nagging fears to let the manifestation come through. Manifestation of the desires you pray for come only from God, and only through your mind's acceptance. There is absolutely no other way.

An acquaintance of mine questioned this premise: "I don't go along with that at all," he said. "It doesn't work, and I can prove it. Take me. I've tried and tried to get rid of this cough. As a last resort, I tried prayer. You say I have to believe. I did believe. I really believed God could cure me. But you see I'm still hacking."

"You don't expect God to heal you," I said.

"How can I expect it? I tried it and it didn't work. I'm still coughing."

Another man in the group, who thinks faster than I, spoke up, "How do you know you're not healed? You've never stopped to look." Then he added, "It would help if you stopped smoking, too."

To some, speaking affirmations in prayer may seem ridiculous. To declare something to be true that obviously is not seems the height of futility. At best, some might say it is kidding yourself; at worst, it is hiding your head in the sand instead of facing reality. This concept has its supporters, but Jesus Christ would not have been one of them. He never spoke in negatives. Every statement by Him recorded in the Bible is an affirmation. From the Beatitudes forward and backward, He proclaimed the ideal to be existent, whether or not it was presently manifest. If you would learn how to pray and to live successfully, re-read the words of Jesus Christ.

Pray For, Not Against

This we know: We do not pray for something bad *not* to happen; we pray for something good to *come about.* We do not pray that another person will be restrained from doing something that we believe will harm us or him; instead, we pray that he will be led to do whatever is good for both him and ourselves. We turn the negative over and look at the other side, which is the positive. That we accentuate.

It is clear that our motives play a part in the effectiveness of our prayers. If we pray that something be manifested in our lives that will at the same time work a hardship on another, or take unfair advantage of him, or impose our wishes on him against his will, we pray amiss. This prayer will not be answered, because we cannot believe it should. God, our Creator, placed Himself within each of us, and His nature permeates us and colors the action of our minds with His love. We may deny it, or attempt to bury it beneath an overcrust of pragmatism, but we cannot eradicate it. For example, we cannot accept compassion as weakness, as some may claim it to be, because compassion is natural to us. We can be comfortable only when our thoughts are in consonance with the divine principle of love.

When we pray, let us pray for others as well as ourselves, but for ourselves first. We pray to clear our minds of worldly things, and to lift our consciousness to attunement with the pure, clean mind of God. In this rarified atmosphere we can effectually pray for another person. Our prayers should be that our neighbor be healed, prospered, and led by divine intelligence within to follow the course that is for his highest good. That is the extent of our involvement in his affairs. Some persons may feel this is no involvement at all, but let us know that our neighbor has available the same higher intelligence that we have, the same right to live his own life, the same freedom to think, to analyze, to decide.

He has the same right to make mistakes and thereby learn. We need to go our own way and keep our own fences mended; as for him, *"Unbind him and let him go."* (John 11:44) Advise perhaps, impose our will, never!

Each of us is by nature a praying person. Our God-inspired minds tell us that we should pray, and that, when we pray aright, our every good desire will come to pass. No thing, situation, or problem can successfully withstand the power of prayer!

Having learned to pray successfully, we reap the rewards of peace, joy, and abundance that we were born to attain. We have a divine right to fulfillment of our every need. All-powerful God wills it so.

How do we know what is rightfully ours? How do we know the thing we desire is good for us? How do we recognize the kind of prayer that brings the answer we need?

Get Acquainted with God

If you do not feel comfortable, expectant, and at ease with God when you pray, perhaps you ought to get better acquainted. You cannot pray to a void. You cannot pray with any degree of involvement to a white cloud of mystery of which you have little understanding. God is God, not a superstition.

You especially cannot pray successfully to a God of whom you are afraid. Passages in the Bible tell us to fear God or fear Jehovah, but surely this does not mean that His name ought to strike dread in our hearts. Let us look for a more rational meaning of fear as applied to the God we know as love.

Charles Fillmore wrote that, when used in this context, fear takes the dictionary definition: *Awe, reverence, especially for the*

Supreme Being. Our religion should be logical, and this meaning surely is logical.

However, people who approach God in fear (frightful) are likely to pray to appease or propitiate Him rather than to commune with a non-judgmental Father who is ever within and about them as absolute good. This kind of fear is a debilitating emotion. It robs us of confidence and faith. It builds a wall of separation between us and God. Fear blinds us to our Father's true nature and chills the warmth of His presence within our consciousness. When we are subject to fear, we are as *slaves who fear to speak.* Edmund Burke said: *No passion so effectually robs the mind of all its powers of acting and reasoning as fear;* and nothing robs our prayers of their dynamic effectiveness so completely as fear of God. There can be no true communion with Him if our minds are inhibited or made self-conscious by being afraid. There is total freedom in prayer. To pray aright, pray to Him without thought of the propriety of your prayers, or whether or not you think He is willing to listen.

You may say, "Don't be ridiculous. I'm not afraid of God!" When you pray, do you visualize God as a loving Spirit who desires to supply your every need, or as august Omnipotence? Do you feel that He is too busy to bother with your small problem, or does not want to give you your desired answer because you do not deserve it? How do you regard Him—as a divine Being earnestly desiring to heal, bless, and prosper you, or as one whom you must convince? Do you love God because you love the good He is, or because you believe He expects it, demands it? These are valid questions, and perhaps they will lead you into knowing whether or not you fear all-powerful God. Since the manifestation of your desires comes out of your own higher consciousness, which is the Christ within, one thing is needed—that your mind be open, not constricted by even a subliminal sense of fear. The good you unexpectedly receive comes through the same channel—a prayerful attitude.

God Always Answers

God will reassure you in your meditations. He is waiting to be heard, waiting to tell you and anyone who will listen, that He is ever available to transform sickness into health, lack into abundance, desires into fulfillment.

As far back as Genesis, Abraham heard Him: *After these things the word of the Lord came to Abram in a vision, "Fear not, Abram, I am your shield; your reward shall be very great."* (Gen. 15:1)

This is not to say that because you may pray timidly God will not answer your prayers. He answers every prayer to the degree you permit; but when your mind is filled with fear or doubt, the channel for your good is narrowed accordingly. When you let your mind run free, you are open to the inspiration that He sees you as perfection in all your ways. He is eternally working to fulfill His concept of you. Your good inevitably flows through the channel of your faith, and when you develop a pure faith, *"as a grain of mustard seed,"* (Matt. 17:20) the way becomes clear for Him to overflow your life with His blessings.

Acquaintance with the nature of God eliminates fear. Turn within to the wise and benign Counselor who is seeking to guide you into a permanent and personal paradise of fulfilled dreams. In such communion you will speak to Him not in trepidation or uncertainty but with reverence, respect, and love. His exalted state as the Supreme Being,

Creator of all that is or shall be, arouses awe, but awe unadulterated by fear. This adds to the effect of your prayer, because you know you are touching a greater power than your own physical power, which itself increases your faith. Without faith there is no manifestation.

How to Know God

All of us need to know God. Perhaps we cannot know Him as intimately as He knows us, but we need to know something of His nature; we must know, at least dimly, what omnipotence means. We must come to realize the convergence of His almightiness with our as yet unmanifested needs, producing a relationship of complete integration.

We know God through His works. The good that flows daily into our lives reveals Him at work in our behalf. The seeming miracles that happen to us when all appears hopeless tell of His protecting, healing, harmonizing, prospering presence ever constant in our affairs.

According to Webster, a miracle is: *An event or effect in the physical world deviating from the known laws of nature or transcend-*

ing our knowledge of those laws. We know that the laws of nature do not change, but we also know that, when our human understanding does not reach all the way to the truth, an auspicious outcome of a challenge may, in our view, be a miracle. Such miracles are always happening. We are suddenly saved from a dire consequence when our own efforts have been fruitless; at the last moment, when disaster is imminent, we are delivered from a situation of lack by an unexpected inflow of money; we are rescued, healed, or liberated in circumstances that in our opinion seemed to offer little hope. If we will recognize these wondrous occurrences as works of God, how our faith will grow! Miracles are more easily indentified in situations of stress or danger than in more commonplace circumstances, but they occur no more regularly in one than in the other.

A few years ago, my wife Cecil and I traveled in a twenty-foot freight canoe 2,000 miles down the Yukon River, nearly from its beginning to its end, through Canada and Alaska. The work of God was clearly evident countless times during this three-month voyage. We experienced miracle after miracle.

Absolute neophytes that Cecil and I were,

our successful passage through Five Fingers Rapids was a certain miracle. Five Fingers is a fabled hazard in the Yukon, the scene of many disastrous wrecks and some fatalities during the Klondike gold rush. Our canoe was tossed about in the violent rapids like a chip in a stormy sea, completely out of control. We did not capsize, our canoe did not bury itself permanently as it dived again and again into huge troughs, and we were not swamped; indeed, we were carried safely through with nothing more serious than a drenching and six inches of water in the bottom of our craft.

Later we found our way through the uncharted and dreaded Yukon Flats, a 300-mile wilderness in which the big river spreads out to as much as six miles wide, and is choked with a maze of heavily forested islands. It is a region of treacherous currents, submerged gravel bars, dead-end sloughs, and pockets of debris. Over all, there is a great loneliness.

Quicksand!

During the trip, I refilled the gasoline tank of our outboard motor on shore from the reserve supply so I would not spill gasoline into the canoe. One afternoon I pulled in to shore for this purpose. The flat beach, a rarity on the river, looked inviting. The shore fell off slowly into the water, and the canoe ran aground six feet away from the shore. With the gasoline tank and the reserve can in hand, I got out of the boat into ankle-deep water. The river bottom was firm gravel. I should have been warned by the bare, black mud of the beach that showed not a leaf or blade of grass. In my ignorance I advanced up the beach, and my feet sank ominously. I was stopped as though I had run into a wall. My feet were solidly rooted. I was unable to withdraw them from the mud and, indeed, they were slowly sinking. By this time, my legs were buried above my knees. I confess to a certain panic. Cecil, much frightened, held out a paddle in a desperate attempt to help, but the tip was inches beyond my reaching fingers.

I do not actually know how I escaped the quicksand, but I somehow plowed through, an inch at a time, and at last found myself back at the canoe, sweating and exhausted. I am convinced that a miracle happened that sunny afternoon.

During our months of travel on the Yukon, many situations of potential and imminent disaster came and went with what in retrospect seems a minimum of complications. Like the time our canoe grounded solidly on a gravel bar in the middle of the river. We were surrounded by deep water a few feet away. I stood knee-deep in icy water for an hour and a half shoveling gravel from beneath the boat, without a sign of success. It seemed we would be stuck there forever. There was little traffic on the river, so we might have gone undiscovered for days. I had to brace myself against the swift current. Suddenly, without warning or seeming reason, the canoe shot forward, and I had to leap for it or be left behind. A small miracle? It looked enormous to me at the time.

It was somewhat of a miracle that I was able to talk Cecil into embarking on the trip in the first place. She had never been in a canoe and shuddered at the prospect of entrusting her life to it on a big wilderness river with its treacherous currents and rapids. You might also consider it miraculous that she later lost her fear of the canoe and came to love the Yukon.

God is truly a present help in every need. It takes only brief reflection to recall instances in your life when you walked through foreboding circumstances unscathed. Consider the countless times you have been saved from harm, or led into a new and better course, healed of sickness, prospered, or harmonized. Help appeared before you from sources and in ways you could not have foreseen or planned. With this background of fortuitous and happy experiences, why should you continue to fear for your safety or well-being, or for the successful outcome of your undertaking?

Let us learn about God so we may understand something of His works. We need to discover for ourselves a perception of His cryptic nature that is an amalgam of love, authority, power, omniscience, and intelligence. All our lives we have been in Him, and He in us, and we know Him not. Because He is invisible to our mortal eyes and beyond the reach of our hearing, we see Him and hear His voice only in the depths of consciousness. That which each of us sees and hears of Him becomes an individual interpretation that results in varying concepts. One person may see Him as a man with a form much like ours—an old man with a long beard, alternately stern and benign, stationed in a city with gold streets in heaven. This is a comforting image to those who can relate best to a

God "with skin on," or to an all-powerful Being who can understand human problems. And now we find Him jokingly referred to as "She," with an undercurrent of seriousness. Why not? God is as much feminine as masculine—Father-Mother God.

In metaphysics we see Him as everywhere-present Spirit without limitation or form or human emotions. He transcends the foibles and fallacies of mankind. In this pragmatic age we can readily understand why some persons find it troublesome to accept a God without form or human senses or an emotional mind such as ours, and to believe in Him as impersonal Spirit permeating every atom in the universe and existing as intangible qualities such as love, power, will, divine law, abundance, health, and all-good. Try thinking of Him also in another way—as a personal, comforting warmth that envelops you in folds of love and perfect security. In Him you live and move and have your being. You move about in the body of God that is within and surrounding you. You are the body of God extruded and personalized.

Contained in this body in which you are totally immersed is every gift of good you can dream of, ready for your call.

Do you yearn for a personal God? What is more personal than Spirit within you whose sole purpose is to bless, protect, heal, and lead you into a perfect life-style? He is your one-of-a-kind God; you are His one-of-a-kind creation. Wherever you go, He is with you. Whatever you do, He is beside you. He never turns away from you. God is inextricably a part of you, and you of Him; therefore, you are love, authority, energy, health, and abundance, because God is all these. As your hands and feet are parts of you, so are the qualities of God woven into your being. Although some of His divine attributes may appear presently quiescent, they are vitally alive and ready to spring forth at your call to transform your life.

God is First Cause, the Creator of all that is. He is not only creative, He is creativity. Creativity ever stirs within your mind. It is a well-used quality that is the springboard of all your daily activities. Those who have developed their natural creativity to a great degree rise to great heights of accomplishment. Perhaps they may take personal credit and gain honor in the eyes of the world, but it is more to their credit that they listened to the Spirit of creativity within them and utilized another of their divine character-istics—courage. Great orators, scientists, writers, artists, and people in business have developed creativity to a high state, and in their memoirs many of them give credit where it is due, although all do not call it God. Mark Twain claimed that if he could but get the first sentence of a manuscript down on paper, all he had then to do was to let the story write itself. He simply served as a recorder, taking down what he heard in his mind. Other writers have marveled at the in-explicable rush of words and ideas that erupt out of the depths of their consciousness. In-ventors tell of having been directed or prod-ded along an untried course in the develop-ment of an idea. The great artist's brush is guided by an unseen hand in the creation of his masterpiece. What is all this but creativ-ity? And creativity is God.

To those unaccustomed to prayer, God ap-pears to be a stranger, no doubt a rather frightening stranger. No one is impelled to pray unless he believes he is talking to, or communing with, or appealing to a power greater than his own. People are led to pray because of a need, often only when all else has failed. One who is unacquainted with the nature of God logically believes that a divine Being possessing the quintessential ability to satisfy all our needs must be an august God indeed. God looms huge and awesome to that person, a darkly mysterious concentration of power and authority—one to approach discreetly—a heavenly body above and beyond an earthling's understanding.

Sense of Separation

How can a mere man or woman get close to a God like that? This has given rise to a sense of separation between God and man. When prayers are not answered in the same terms as the request, we spring to the belief that God will say no as readily as He says yes. This idea of God may remain with people all their lives.

Yet God answers prayer. In His love He provides yes answers to heartfelt prayers when even a little faith is brought to bear. There is no capriciousness in His answers. He does not decide He will say yes one time and no another. You decide—your attitude, your belief, your acceptance decide. Divine Mind works in immutable law; you work under law. Work with the law and you will inevitably manifest the results prescribed by the law. There are no exceptions, no partial answers, no maybes.

When we elevate our consciousness to a synergetic relationship with God, all the discrete phases of one being are raised to new pinnacles of individual and collective excellence. They remain steadfast and continue under divine grace to express their nature so long as we maintain collaboration with Divine Mind. This is absolute, unalterable, because it is law. Work with His law of faith in the good, and good will be with you and remain with you for all time.

Wavering Faith

George Jackson spent more than half a lifetime learning the nature of God. George Jackson is not his name, but it is one I will use for this purpose. George did not know he was trying to learn about the nature of God; he was simply trying to get along and earn a living. He had highs and lows, and he did not know why.

George ran a small business in a medium-sized town in a Midwestern state. He was not in dreadful straits; he had never been bankrupt, and he had never been in jail. Also, he had never been easy in his mind about his finances or the future of his business. He constantly teetered between confidence and insecurity. When I first met him, I saw a short, bulky man with a round face and light hair that was thinning on top. He had wide, blue, vulnerable eyes that looked at me through steel-rimmed glasses. His wide mouth was quick to grin, and just as quick to sag in melancholy. Once I got to know him well, he liked to fill me in on the formidable complications that went along with running a small business—skyrocketing prices and competition from other businesses. "They give me fits," he lamented, "with their big stocks of goods. They can sell rings around me . . . and their credit! But even if I had their big line of credit it wouldn't do me any good, because I can't sell enough in this little store to make it worthwhile. And I can't afford a bigger place. I'm stuck smack in the middle."

Now and then he made a big sale and was guardedly elated, because he believed that a dry spell was bound to follow. George could usually tell when he was about to have a good day. First, he felt good, like getting out of bed in a warm glow on a sunny morning; second, he felt intuitively that it was about time for another big day; also, the previous day had always been an encouraging one. His happy day was assured if the morning paper hinted at an upturn in business for the current quarter, even if the upturn might be indicated for the East Coast, far from his dusty town. He would march into his small store bright-eyed and expectant. Always a customer would come in and express an interest in a big-ticket item. George would go carefully and thoroughly into his sales story, not pushing or pressuring. The customer would listen attentively. More often than not, the customer would complain about treatment he had gotten at a discount store, or perhaps he would mention that a friend had recommended George's place of business. George would turn on his confident personality and secure the sale.

It was not unusual for several such customers to enter his store on such a day, even two at a time, and the cramped building would be alive with business activity. When it came time to go home, George would be high. He'd had a big day. But the next morning he would be settled back into a more moderate state of mind, grateful for yesterday's business, but believing that such things run in cycles and he could not expect a recurrence for a while.

Expectations Manifest

Expectation and manifestation are twins so inextricably integrated that they might be called one. When one is present, the other is not far away. Expectation and acceptance are synonymous, and long ago we learned that what we accept in consciousness we receive. God's good goes where it is wanted, needed, and accepted. You draw to yourself positive answers to prayer through the creative process working in your consciousness. Come fully into the realization that God knows your needs before you do; it was He who implanted the desire into your mind. He wants you to have fulfillment. You must expect, accept, and by all means ask.

Is this idea nullified by the fact that unexpected blessings, even miracles, appear in our lives? Not at all. An expectant frame of mind brings not only the good you pray for but other good as well. Similar effects seem to follow one another. Seldom does a stroke of good fortune come into our lives unattended by others. Does something suddenly occur "out of the blue" when we have done nothing at all to cause it to come forth? Not quite, as reflection will prove. Perhaps we did not expect a specific blessing that came to us, but we had developed a consciousness of expectation of good. God answers prayers, or prayerful attitudes, in ways that are often better than we know or dare to outline.

George Jackson called himself a God-fearing man. He did not fear God in the way he feared bankruptcy, or incurable illness, or rattlesnakes, but he felt the necessity of being very careful in his dealings with Him. He would not deliberately offend God, and in general he tried to do what he thought God wanted him to do. He read passages from the Bible when time permitted, and meanwhile he felt guilty for not reading the Bible more frequently. He went to church twice a month and sang lustily when the pastor announced a hymn. George was sincere in his religion, and he had certainly earned a good reputation in town as a businessman who would not cheat you. He blessed the food at the dinner table and, when he went to bed, he repeated a long prayer, memorized from a book years before.

George was, by all the world's standards, a

good man. He worked hard and made a decent living for his family, although he was never able to accumulate enough money to consider himself well-to-do, or even secure. "God," he would say, "doesn't want me to be rich."

At last he arrived at a partial realization—to bring a repeat of his good business days, he must first reproduce the conditions. He dared to maintain a sense of expectancy, although he never lost the uncomfortable feeling that he was somehow trying to fool God. Nevertheless he learned that things do not just happen, people make them happen, allow them to happen.

We must all come to accept the fact that being a "good man" or "good woman" is not enough. It does not automatically guarantee that one will henceforth and forevermore abide in heaven, either somewhere in the sky or on Earth. The rank of *good man* is a result, not a cause. The terms *good man* and *good woman* are nomenclature of society. Being a good man or a good woman is important and requires strong discipline and a commendable regard for one's fellows; but as Martin Luther said more than four centuries ago: *Good deeds do not a Christian make.*

God is not changeable, nor jealous, nor is He subject to interpretation. God is Principle, Law. His law is eternal and immutable. He does not adapt to changing times or morals or civilizations. He is constancy itself. He implanted His law prominently in our inward parts in the beginning, and we may read it again in our meditations any time we choose. He also gave us unrestricted freedom to live by the law or to go apart from it.

The Law Defined

In Matthew 22:37-40, Jesus Christ defined the law and set it before us as our guide, our authority and fulfillment: *"You shall love the Lord your God with all your heart, and with all your soul, and with all your mind. This is the great and first commandment. And a second is like it, you shall love your neighbor as yourself. On these two commandments depend all the law and the prophets."*

Only Jesus attained the full measure of at-one-ment with Divine Principle, or Law, and He demonstrated dominion over time, space, matter, mortality, and his own humanness. Others before and since Jesus appeared on Earth have reached varying levels of understanding, and demonstrated accordingly. To-day, as always, we reap the benefits of divine munificence to the extent that we follow the rules.

God has no favorites. Men and women blessed with health, riches, intellect, talent, and happiness have found the way to the treasures of Spirit, but not through a fortu-itous and exclusive relationship with the Giver of all gifts. God is Father of all—the rich and poor and in-between, the Catholics, Jews, Presbyterians, Lutherans, Methodists, Baptists, Buddhists, Taoists, Unity stu-dents, and all other religions, including those who profess not to believe in God. You had your beginning in Him, and you are sustained by divine love.

God placed His representative Self within each of His manifestations to remain *closer than hands and feet*, expressing His qualities through us into the world. Creativity, along with all other divine attributes, is strong within everyone. Creativity works in our con-sciousness and in our intellect, not only to develop our understanding and to perfect our affairs, but to build our bodies and construct our environment. Let us remember that cre-ativity is none other than God.

Jesus maintained that the first great commandment is that we love God, which is to say, the law. This connotes that we are to obey the law. The second is that we love our neighbor. A stumbling block in our understanding of this biblical passage is that we may point to persons about us who appear to demonstrate a superabundance of good, yet who, in our view, fail to pass the first test. In their seemingly un-Christlike way of living, we can see no evidence of love of God, and it is clear that they have no love for their neighbor. In our small understanding, perhaps tinged with jealousy, we are likely to look upon them as selfish, greedy, unfeeling, unpleasant people, yet they manifest the good things of life to a far greater extent than we do. We question: How can this be in accord with Jesus Christ's first and great commandment? The inference of His commandment is that, if we fail to love God and our neighbors, we place ourselves outside the circle of blessings of Divine Mind.

This question is important to our understanding of Spirit. God, we readily agree, encompasses every imaginable good in the realm of the ideal, and good is constantly available to us to the degree that we ask—

health, wealth, wisdom, love, abundance, and all other qualities that constitute the Supreme Being. All are potentially ours, individually and collectively. One may love wealth with all one's heart and inevitably manifest great material riches, yet be unhappy in other areas. One may feel alone and unloved, constantly embroiled in personal and career problems because he has failed to accept other gifts of God as part of his consciousness.

That which you love manifests; that which you deny is denied you. So love the good and deny evil.

Everyone who prays asks for something. Even when you pray for others, you ask God to provide something that is not now evident. This bothers many people. "I'm always asking," they say. "God is going to get sick and tired of my eternal begging for this or that." This comes from an erroneous concept of God, an idea of an emotional God who thinks as they do, one who makes affirmative or negative decisions about their requests. Do you find it easier to pray for the health and welfare of another person than for your own? Are you troubled and embarrassed to ask for a windfall to pay a pressing bill, yet feel you are acting the part of a good Christian when you pray earnestly for the prosperity of your neighbor who is in need?

This brings us to other questions: Do you believe that God loves someone else more than you? Are you not the beloved child of your Creator? You share with Jesus Christ and every other person the potential Sonship that is the ideal. Jesus attained the potential; you are on your way, and that makes you divine. You, and your brother, and your neighbor, and the person on the other side of the world are equal in the sight of God. You may think of the other person as a better Christian, one of whom God no doubt approves highly. Let me remind you: God approves of you both! You and all others are His sons with whom He is well pleased. Your acquaintance with God will have revealed by now that He does not hold your failings against you. His love is great enough to envelop all of us equally.

You need have no hesitancy in asking God to give you the desires of your heart. God is love; it is His nature to give. He has been giving to us all our lives, throughout eternity. At this point in our unfoldment we are unable to stretch our minds far enough to encompass the extent of His givingness. He gave us life; He gave us Himself. He gave us all that we are and have. And we feel His presence saying that He will, in His love, give to us freely all that we shall ever have or be. He can do no less than continue to pour blessings without ceasing from His storehouse of good.

Think of yourself as moving through a highly charged atmosphere in whose atomic structure rests every unmanifested desire. This atmosphere is the body of God in whom we " '. . . *live and move and have our being.*' " (Acts 17:28) Within you, outside of you, above, and below you, and further than your mind can reach, everywhere evenly present, the body of God holds and protects you. It is the everlasting arms of His love. You are immersed in everything you will ever need or want. State your claim and it is yours. You open the gates to the inflow of treasures by praying the prayer of faith.

This is not simplistic. It is fact; it is law. It has its own rules that inevitably work to bring the manifestation. The rules are fulfilled in prayer. Pray rightly and you touch God in a collaborative process of demonstration. Praying rightly does not necessarily mean that you recite a formal opus that has been laboriously worked out during hours of cudgeling your brain to find the right words, or one that someone you respect has previously written. God is not impressed by fine words. There is not a more powerful prayer, for all its simplicity, than: *I claim my oneness with God my Father,* when your mind is charged with the meaning of the prayer. Pray simply, in everyday language; pray with heartfelt conviction; pray with love and joyous expectancy. Above all, pray with faith. Pray with thanksgiving. God does not require your thanks, but you need to give it because giving thanks strengthens your faith that you have received the answer to your prayer. God is impersonal. He is Spirit, unquestioning love. Prepare your consciousness to receive, and align yourself with Divine Mind, by praise and thanksgiving.

Everyone needs to get acquainted with God. Draw close to Him in understanding and open new worlds of His treasures. Know Him, not only as omnipresent, omniscient, and omnipotent God, but also as your loving Father who is available every moment to satisfy your every desire with abundance beyond your most extravagant dreams. It requires only that you ask aright!

Get Acquainted with Yourself

After living with ourselves for many years, it would seem that we should know the person inside full well—every weakness and strength, every whim, every quirk. But some of us have consistently downgraded our worth, which proves that we do not know ourselves very well. We have experienced failure so many times, have been wrong so many times, have demonstrated less than we feel we should have so many times that we have privately concluded that we are not too smart. Beneath the swagger and bluster on the surface is, in some of us, a self-disparaging being who concedes he is less a person than he purports to be or ought to be. This is a creeping negativism that spreads into every area of our lives and produces a sense of insecurity. We have no real reason to feel insecurity, but fear saddles us with a debilitating lack of assurance.

This installment in this book on prayer is not intended as a psychiatric treatment but simply as an examination of facts to arrive at the truth of who and why we are.

Let us begin with an understanding that while we are all one in Spirit, each is individual in manifestation. It is important that we consider this when we talk about ourselves and our approach to prayer. Prayer is not a mechanical process. It cannot be laid out with a slide rule and protractor to serve as a model to fit everyone, because everyone is different. Not only are we unlike one another in background, attitude, and degree of awareness, but we stand alone in our needs and desires. Of course we all want health and prosperity, peace of mind and harmonious relationships, but specifics differ widely with every individual. Wealth is not satisfying if it is not gained and maintained in a satisfying way. Health loses its savor if it is coupled with fear of its being lost. We all want different things and different ramifications of things. Not only do our needs vary from another's, but they change from day to day.

We react to a circumstance in a manner exclusive to ourselves. We look fruitlessly for a hard and fast procedure for prayer, but there are no hard and fast procedures for it. Like reading glasses, a prayer suited to one person will not fit another. Many people find no real release in group prayers but must go apart and pray alone; others find the support of a group to be helpful.

Even so, the general aspects of prayer are universal. We need to pray to align ourselves with the wisdom and power of the cosmos. We all want to pray for the joy that is in it. Our nature demands that we make an assertive effort to fill any kind of void in our lives. Praying is a means of gratifying that inner demand. Perhaps we are surprised when prayer turns out to be the catalyst for the solution. We must keep reminding ourselves that prayers are always answered, and always in the manner in which we ask. *"You will decide on a matter, and it will be established for you . . . ."* (Job 22:28) Everyone who asks receives. We receive exactly what we ask for. But everyone does not always receive what is wanted.

To pray successfully we must observe certain general rules. After we have learned to understand why we pray and to whom we pray, then we must come to understand ourselves. The profound complexities of our nature are astounding, far beyond those revealed in casual perception. An analysis will convince us that we are not experts regarding our own nature. We may not have thought about it much, or we may have buried deep in our consciousness some of the "failings" we have discovered in ourselves. For example, shyness. We might cure this trait if we would but realize that it had its rise and obtains present sustenance from a false belief in our unworthiness.

Do not believe that you are of little worth. Some may advise: "Be humble. That's the way to be Godlike. Jesus said the meek are blessed." Humility is admirable, but not self-abasement. To be meek does not mean to be spineless. And having confidence in yourself does not have to take you on an ego trip. Always remember that you are a spiritual being. You share with all others an equal and great worth in the world.

Plato said: *The unexamined life is not worth living.* I do not believe it is beneficial to our progress to launch a perennial and exhaustive examination of our every thought, reaction, and attitude. But self-examination of a rational kind is helpful and in fact needed for our self-image and peace of mind. Discovery that we are not the inept persons that we may have thought ourselves to be can transform our lives. It will give us a new perspective on persons and circumstances and our relationship to them.

Look for the positive rather than the negative in yourself. Enumerate your strengths, deny your weaknesses, and the weaknesses will eliminate themselves. Take a good look at what you actually are, if not presently, then in attainable potential, and you will feel a resurgence of power and faith in yourself. You will know that you are, in Truth, unbeatable. Your inheritance from your Father is a natural capability equal to any task or challenge you will ever be called upon to face. The Spirit within you urges you to meet circumstances rather than postpone them. Confrontation with the world is your opportunity to prove again and again that by means of your native talents you can emerge successful. Understand this and you know you are the qualified person you have always wanted to be. By nature you are proficient, intelligent, and goal-reaching. The only thing in your life that denies this Truth is your negative concept of yourself.

Simply and surely you are the beloved son and heir of almighty Father-Mother God. With this royal inheritance there is nothing to fear. Your dominion is ordained and complete. Consider yourself a divine being only a little lower than the angels. You were given authority over your affairs by divine pronouncement, but a prerequisite to exercising this authority is command of your mind.

Why Problems?

Question: Why do we have problems? Answer: Perhaps because we provide them with a secure and comfortable home.

Inevitably we attract evil by holding it in consciousness, thinking about it, expecting it. Fortunately, we attract good in the same manner. We attract evil by fearing it; we attract good by loving it. We are free to accept or reject our inheritance of treasures of mind, body, and affairs. If we reject them, either through choice or ignorance, there is no possible way those treasures can manifest. If we choose to dedicate ourselves to acceptance, there is no way our joy and fulfillment can escape manifestation.

No one in his right mind will deliberately invite problems into his life. It logically follows that when we have a problem—first, we have invited it and, second, we are not in our right minds. Let us define the right mind. It is the illumined mind, the positive mind. The wrong mind is the frightened, doubting, negative mind.

No one wants the wrong mind, but our minds play tricks on us. Do you realize that it is easier to be negative than positive? When we are rebuffed, it is easier to be angry than forgiving because to forgive, we must first work to get pride out of the way. When a catastrophic misfortune, or even a minor one, becomes imminent (because of a wrong mind), it is easier to go along with the appearance than to meet it with a healthy, constructive attitude. We miss the opportunity to dissolve the misfortune before it envelops us. When the disaster has succeeded in getting past our lazy defenses, our problem-conditioned minds say resignedly that such crises are always bouncing around and some are bound to hit us. Thus, we work to excuse our failures. While some of us may fight problems bitterly, we frequently do so with less than genuine expectations. "That is the way the world is," we sigh. "It is contentious, devious, and always pursuing us with evil." All this to spare ourselves the responsibility for an unending succession of crises, as well as for the real effort needed to steer our wills toward command. It is never easy to break a habit. Redirecting a thought pattern is like breaking up housekeeping and starting for a new land.

Sooner or later we must take control of our minds and affairs. It may appear impractical to expect our stubborn minds to lift themselves out of waywardness, but mind is a marvelous instrument. If an idea is exciting enough, it catches on and is incorporated into the mind's structure. If the glamour fades later, our thoughts are just as quick to drop the idea and return to their accustomed ways.

In that regard, it is important to remember that our habitual thoughts are the builders behind every condition manifest in our lives. Nothing happens to us that did not first happen in our minds. As we think, so we are. This is so common as to have become trite, yet it is nonetheless true.

Our minds are in eternal contact with the

Mind of God. Our minds *are* the Mind of God, one and the same, personalized. In them is involved the full gallery of divine qualities— creative power, love, strength, wisdom, and all others.

Every Thought a Prayer

Prayer is defined as communion with God. It is a transference of ideas within the one Mind. Even though you may not want it to be, your every thought is a prayer. All the power of heaven is directed toward its manifestation. Obviously, every thought does not spring into manifestation, thank God. But every thought makes its mark, and enough marks make a picture. The picture is the manifestation. A thought held in mind without being opposed by contrary thoughts is bound to come forth. Whether the thought is something you desire or something you fear, the effect is the same. It is ever working its way toward its destiny of becoming real and true in your affairs.

This is not to say that prayer effects must necessarily evolve through a period of time. Jesus Christ performed instantaneous healings. He performed miracles of every kind, all without waiting. The requirement of elapsed time is the invention of man, because we cannot believe our good can happen so quickly. On occasion many of us have seen our prayers answered swiftly, even before our asking. Some of us tend to believe that if our prayers are answered at once, the same result was about to happen anyway and our prayer was not needed.

If it is the thought in mind that manifests, how does one account for the many things that happen of which we had no idea? Attitudes of good produce good. Prayerful thoughts, good thoughts, happy thoughts, grateful, loving, and confident thoughts form into a powerful attitude of faith that not only attracts but opens the way for an inflow of miracles. Somewhere in consciousness rests the idea that manifests. When we maintain an attitude of faith, we may look for the appearance of our specific desire and expect other miracles as well. Everything goes to him who has faith, love, a grateful heart, him who has expectancy of marvelous things happening to him today, tomorrow, and every day.

Happy conditions follow naturally after a train of positive thoughts; misfortune follows negative thoughts. You make all the decisions about your life, not your boss, not your spouse, not your family, not the price of gold, nor the degree of inflation, nor what happens in Europe, or the Middle East, or the Orient. It is all done in your powerful, ever-active, creative mind.

There is much work to be done in the world, and everyone has a part in it. To keep the multitudinous affairs of the world—God's world—moving requires an infinitude of individual acts. In order to maintain essential balance, each of the vast numbers of functions must be performed in an individual way. If everyone acted in the same way and thought in the same way, this would be a lopsided world, and life would soon descend into chaos. There are balances and counterbalances, pros and cons, highs and lows, near and far, executives and laborers, housewives and secretaries. For every group there is a counter-group. Only when error succeeds in overbalancing good is there a so-called emergency. Only when great numbers of people become mindlessly polarized in hostility can there be wars.

You are the microcosm of the universe, the drop of water in the ocean which contains all that is in the whole. In you are divergent concepts and the intelligence to discern right. In you are warring factions and the power to bring agreement and peace. In your mind are strength and weakness, health and sickness, success and failure, joy and despair. There is also in you dominion over the negative aspects of your being and the ability to replace them with good. Above all, in you is God, by whose sole authority you build a life of fulfillment and freedom, and eliminate imperfection from your affairs, no matter how frighteningly evil may loom before you. This is a part of ourselves that is difficult for many of us to realize and accept—the part that is divine, that is capable, that knows no other master than our Higher Self, which is the Christ.

Through the power of the Christ we are emancipated from subjugation to the changing whims of the world. We are freed from fear and want and all misfortune.

You attain the realization of your divinely capable Self through prayer. In prayer you contact God, and He reassures you, counsels you, strengthens you, as His great love takes hold of your mind. Prayer is the elevator to your happiness and dominion; it takes you home to your true Self which is one with the authority of God.

Our Own Perfect Place

No one can be happy if he feels his life is contributing nothing to the world. But there is a true place for you, and you are now abiding in it. Tomorrow there may be a different place, and you will live in it. Your happiness is gauged by the extent to which you express the potential that was born in you. You have known your potential since the beginning. It is what you would most like to do or be. It is not what appears most glamorous or exciting, or what someone else says you should do, or what sounds the most profitable. It is that which gives you the greatest sense of fulfillment when you think of attaining it.

One of life's greatest frustrations is striving to be a captain of industry when you would rather be an artist, or struggling to become a world-renowned physicist when you would prefer to grow wheat. You can be happy composing a symphony or building a kitchen chair, if you are suited to musical composition or furniture building. Who is to say which adds more to the total of human existence? In today's society, the emphasis seems to be on education. The belief is that everyone should attend a university and get a PhD or at least a Master's degree. Attainment of these goals may have an effect on one's social position but not necessarily on one's happiness.

I believe one person can be as happy baking a cake as another is writing a poem. An exalted position in industry, or the arts, or politics carries high prestige and may open doors to wealth and influence, but it has nothing to do with permanent joy. Other things determine that, such as interests, talents, and bent of mind.

The nature of the job you are to do should be a private decision. This is one phase of life in which we should not bow to another's urging. Bow only to God. Let Him reveal your potential and the means of attaining it. He is always right. All your life you have lived with a desire in your heart to do or be something, and that something is what you are naturally best equipped to be. It is a gift of God.

If you are undecided about how to occupy your time or how to earn a living, go to God. Go apart in quiet prayer and wait. If the answer does not come at once, try again. Never forget that you are the child of omniscient God. He knows all there is to know about you, much more than you will ever know, and He will guide you to your highest potential. He gave you natural aptitudes, and they have been seeking expression ever since.

No Stone Unturned

If your potential goal is such that it will lead you to a place of importance in the public eye, fine; you owe it to God and to yourself to leave no stone unturned. Work for the academic degree if that is needed. Climb whatever ladder appears before you. You will be happy in the seeking, exultant in the accomplishment. If your potential lies in another direction, follow it with all the force at your command. Your ultimate goal is happiness not riches, and they are not necessarily the same thing. Your real desire is for fulfillment not glory, for self-esteem rather than the envy of others. Marching to your own drum is the only way to permanent satisfaction.

Your present age has little to do with your potential accomplishments. If you are young, it may seem that you have a time advantage;

but in God there is no time. Countless documented instances tell of men and women in retirement years who, after having worked a lifetime in unsatisfying jobs, have flung themselves into work they always wanted to do and have gone on to financial success and, for the first time, a sense of peace.

The most important realization you will ever have is that you are a beloved child of God. He gave you the equipment, the opportunity, and the means of achieving happiness. He also gave you freedom, freedom even from His will for you. He is eternally ready as your counselor and guide, but He demands only that you follow your own inner promptings.

Perhaps you feel that you are bound by circumstances. In reality there are no circumstances that can bind you. There is a sure way out of such a sense of constriction, and it is embodied in self-realization. Realize that your adversary is fear, not formidable appearances. You are full heir to the strength of God, in whom there can be no fear or weakness or failure. His heritage makes you divinely capable of doing anything that you are led to do. Impress this Truth firmly into your mind and heart, and you will never need further reassurance of your worth or capability. In prayer are your illumination and strength.

You Can Achieve

Everyone wants to achieve, and everyone can achieve. Even more, everyone wants to be happy, and that takes a special kind of achievement. Take Jeremy Protter, for example. Jeremy Protter was a man whom you did not call Jeremy unless you were a close friend, of whom he had few. No one ever called him Jerry, not even his wife Erline. Jeremy was a morose man with deep lines around his mouth and forehead. He was executive vice-president of a sizeable corporation. The Protters lived in a sprawling house in a suburb with manicured lawns and hedges, and Erline was the best dressed woman at the country club. They had two children—a son and a daughter. Both were married and living at a distance, and both were well-to-do, but not particularly happy. The family got together infrequently.

After dinner one evening, Jeremy dropped his bomb. He had eaten sparingly of late because of his ulcers. "I'm resigning my job," he said with little emotion.

Erline smiled. He had made noises like this before, but nothing had ever come of it.

"I made up my mind today," he continued. "I'm sick of the rat race. I'm tired of fighting. I've been fighting all my life." He knew she wasn't really listening, but he went on anyway. "I had to fight first to get where I am and, for the last ten years, to stay there. I'm quitting." He gave her a sidelong glance.

"Why?"

"I just told you why. I've had enough."

This was beginning to sound serious. "What do you propose to do?" she asked uncertainly.

"I'm going to sell this place, buy a farm, and raise chickens."

"Chickens!" she said shrilly. Then she laughed. Jeremy would look funny in overalls.

"You can't do that," she said. Images of their country club friends came into her mind. What would they think? If Jeremy insisted on changing his job, leaving the fine position that had given them prestige and wealth, Erline could think of a lot of businesses he might go into—but chickens!

"I'm going to sell this place. How many

rooms do we need to live in? We've got sixteen rooms in this monstrosity, with a lot of dirt around it doing nothing but looking pretty and eating up money."

Erline was frightened. "But what will happen to me?"

"What do you think will happen to you? You were raised on a farm just as I was. I should have stayed there. I always wanted to run a chicken farm, a real up-to-date, scientific chicken farm with all the modern stuff. I got sidetracked onto this merry-go-round and couldn't get off, afraid to get off. Now I'm cutting loose."

"You'll never do it," Erline said firmly. "You like money too much, and your important job, and your clubs. You'll never give up all that for a dirty chicken farm."

Farm Becomes Reality

Three months later Jeremy and Erline moved to a farm twenty miles out in the country, and Jeremy spent the following months building chicken houses designed to hold 15,000 laying hens, plus brooder houses, incubator houses, storage houses, a shop, and sundry buildings. He sought expert advice from a university, and incorporated the latest procedures into his operation. He crawled into bed exhausted every night. His left thumbnail was continuously discolored from repeated banging with a hammer. He lost forty pounds, along with his ulcer, and loved every minute of it. He was a quarter of a million dollars in debt, but as happy as a small boy on Christmas morning.

Twelve years later Jeremy is past retirement age but has no thought of retiring. "Having too much fun," he says. His expanded facilities are becoming a showplace for poultry ranchers. His house has only six rooms and a bathroom, but it is more comfortable than the big house ever was, although less plush. Jeremy enjoys better health than he has had in thirty years. He gets up each morning eager for the day. Erline too is content. She won first prize with her plum jam at last year's district fair. They have lost some of their former country club friends, but they do not miss them. They have found a lot of new ones, "solid friends," Jeremy calls them. Last year Jeremy's income was more than he had ever earned as a vice-president, but neither he nor Erline consider their personal income as important as they once did. They prefer to put profits back into the business, not to make more money, but just to see the project grow. It is something they are building themselves, just Jeremy and Erline.

Ideas Become Real

You learn about yourself when you give your true nature a chance to come through. Perhaps your priorities change; maybe you see your talents and dreams in a different light; possibly your potential becomes clearer and more logical and probable; certainly your relationships with God and your neighbor and the world are revealed in a new perspective.

Jeremy did not consciously pray for inspiration and strength and guidance. But he prayed, just as you and I pray, every hour of the day. We are so closely tuned to God that our every thought, every earnest desire, comes under the law of Divine Mind. Our minds partake of the creativity of Spirit; every idea that enters moves toward manifestation. Any idea that is entertained consistently will ultimately emerge into form.

Jeremy had wanted money. He had worked

hard for it in the way he thought it had to be acquired and, over a period of years, he succeeded. Then he realized that money was not what he wanted after all, which God had been telling him all the while through Jeremy's nagging desire to own a chicken ranch.

Your own inspiration is as close as the presence of God, *nearer than hands and feet.* It is as close as your mind. It is revealed to you in prayer. Control your thoughts, guard your attitudes, have faith in the verity of your deep desires. You possess illimitable authority over your affairs. You have made your life what it is, and you will make what it will be in the future.

The Devil Made Me Do It

Satan is pictured in medieval demonology as a Mephistophelean figure in red tights, with cloven hoofs, horns, and a long tail, walking upon the Earth and carrying a pitchfork with which to jab people. He is called the chief devil, the overseer of hell, the prince of darkness, Beelzebub, and a great many other such names. Lesser devils are referred to as demons, who flit about seeking unsuspecting people. Many persons believe all this to be the truth.

Actually, Mephistopheles is a principal character in Goethe's "Faust," and he is purely fictional. Johann Wolfgang von Goethe wrote this dramatic poem, one of the most beautiful in literature, in the 18th century, to illustrate his premise that man's soul is ever seeking to express more of the good. Mephistopheles represents Satan, the symbol of the Adversary.

Satan, or the devil, in the Bible was a character of extreme disagreeable qualities. Wherever he went, evil things happened. According to the Talmud—the book of Jewish law—Satan was cast out of heaven for disobedience, and he became a fallen angel, roaming the Earth as an evil being beyond the protection and sanction of God. Milton's Lucifer in "Paradise Lost" follows this theme. Lucifer and Mephistopheles are characters in epic poems, but both are wholly fictional.

Satan and the devil are mentioned numerous times in the Bible, but in each instance the symbolism can be clearly discerned.

Actually, there is only God, the Presence and Power, the Lord, Creator, Sustainer of the universe, the God of all people. I believe that God is love. I also believe that Satan and the devil are only symbols.

Satan is a Hebrew word meaning *adversary*. Because of the strong influence of the race mind in our consciousness, all of us have seeming adversaries in constant attendance. Regardless of their unreality, these adversaries are quite powerful. They are called: willfulness, greed, envy, hate, fear, selfishness, and negativism.

These symbolic devils are manufactured in our minds out of nothingness; they sap our strength and cause us to regard the world as our personal antagonist. They are nothings. But once we think them into being, they are capable of overwhelming us with troubles and suffering. They are, in truth, our only enemies.

In the bright light of understanding we recognize devils as transitory and unreal. They cannot face spiritual discernment, which reveals them to be mere imaginings, totally ineffectual without the power we give them. They are born of our mistaken reactions to events or to other persons. We are their inventors and, logically, their masters.

Devils cannot stand prayer. Expose them to prayer and they will loose their hold on you and fade into oblivion. Rid yourself of the devils of willfulness, greed, envy, hate, fear, selfishness, and negativism and you will emerge into a new world of freedom. Take them for what they are, simply unwise concepts, and call upon God in prayer to cleanse your consciousness of them. See them clearly as the masquerading imposters they are. They are your adversaries and must be eliminated if you are to stand forth as a child of God in outer fact, an achiever, and a happy person.

Pray for understanding and strength, and when you pray, have faith that what you pray for is done. Prayer is your front-line defense against the adversaries.

Overcome Temptation

Jesus Christ was tempted greatly, but because He was rooted in God, He had the spiritual strength to turn away from evil. During our lives, you and I have also successfully resisted temptation, and we have profited accordingly. But at those times when we have failed to follow our higher leadings, we have suffered the inevitable consequences. The proof is clear. When we rise in consciousness and approach even distantly the exalted state of Jesus Christ, we find that temptations have a lessening pull, and we can more easily let them go. Jesus Christ attained a pure consciousness attuned to Spirit and was less subject to worldly temptations. The sooner we realize that life in God leads to freedom, the more quickly we will find joy.

Strength is something for which we need to pray—inner strength to resist temptation. We shall not be wholly happy until we have achieved the strength to seek earnestly the good and pleasant things, and to turn away from error—to develop strength of character. It is the strength of God at the center of our being that knows no weakness, no error, no compromise.

Strength is a moral force that has its foundation in the uncompromising expression of Divine Mind. Its opposite—weakness—is an adversary that sometimes lurks in us as lethargy, fear, or waywardness, and robs us of our divine inheritance. Moral strength is a universal gift of God. Strength of will to resist evil is not affectation but an assertive power that leads to self-control and the attainment of sublime perfection. Resisting error means denial of the negative and affirmation of the positive. That is the way to health, wealth, and eternal joy.

Take positive steps to eliminate your adversaries. Long-standing habits of thought may need to be broken; turnabout of some attitudes may be needed. Certainly a program of vigilance must be maintained to prevent them from creeping back into consciousness after you have discarded them.

The seven devils—willfulness, greed, envy, hate, fear, selfishness, and negativism—are all man-made.

There are lesser devils, let's call them demons, that spring from these seven devils, such as distrust, hopelessness, pride, unbelief, procrastination, and indecision. But when you destroy the leaders, these lesser parasites are rendered powerless. Countless demons serve the major devils in their nefarious campaign to bury us in travail. The nonsensical part is that they do so with our permission. We even invite them into our lives!

Devils and demons are made strong by their success in past encounters with unsuspecting, unenlightened people. These parasites, though formidable, are paper tigers. They have no substance. See them for what they are—delusions. We can eliminate them with understanding through prayer.

Let us examine the seven devils individually, to prove that they have no substance, and then watch them wither into dry husks in the bright sun of reason, and blow away, out of our consciousness forever. With this, we shall stand free!

Willfulness

Willfulness is the first of the seven devils and the most easily recognized. It is always at hand to lead us down the path to dangerous unrestraint. Willfulness is the state of being governed by personal will without reason, propriety, or thought of other persons or even of our own permanent welfare. This adversary has many names. Call it obstinacy, stubbornness, perverseness, mulishness, inflexibility, or waywardness—it answers to all. It is subtle. It gains its power from a common reluctance to being pushed around. Some persons call it weakness to allow themselves to be influenced by another or by a code of social conduct. This is the subtle part of it. What is weakness? It surely is weakness to permit ourselves to be drawn into license or other error, to our own detriment. It is strength when we agree with our higher nature and refuse to allow ourselves to be diverted to injurious ways.

All people have been subject to some form of external constraint, and to be free to do exactly as we wish is the eternal desire of humankind. To be perfectly free in any society, primitive or modern, is an impossibility, but the quest nevertheless continues. In our determination to escape direction from another person or from society we go to exaggerated lengths.

Willfulness is close to our own nature, only a little beyond the boundary of reasonableness. It is easy to excuse, especially in ourselves, the tendency to go one's way, particularly if it is opposite to the common course. This is being independent, we think smugly, an indication of a strong character. It is considered great praise to say about a person, "He is his own man."

Independence is fine; self-sufficiency, to a point, is admirable; freedom is a salutary goal. It is another matter, however, when independence becomes obstinacy, self-sufficiency descends into conceit, freedom burgeons into license.

Willfulness takes a wholesome state of mind and pumps it up into a riot of error. Subtle, devious, and difficult to conquer is this powerful devil. On one hand it hugs the edges of propriety, and on the other it closely skirts the freedom we value so highly. It works in reckless unrestraint. We send it out of our lives when we realize the childishness of submitting to its demands, particularly when we know it has no real authority.

Greed

The devil greed is the symbol of avariciousness, covetousness, and needless desire for personal advantage without thought of another's well-being. Here again, it springs from good stock; it is an exaggeration of one's natural desire to fulfill the promise of good that lies within every person. As sons of God we are blessed with the divine gift of love, which includes the means of manifesting every desire. But it is not a free gift; we are required to do our part, which is to direct our natural aptitudes toward the end we expect, while expressing the divine qualities of faith, love, and integrity.

We must accept our responsibility to our Creator to express to the fullest the potential of His creation in our lives. Life should be joyous, but not without accountability. There is no joy in idleness. The joy is in attainment. We are born not only with a full complement of talents but with the desire to fulfill them. The desire to enjoy the fruits of our special abilities is a natural and commendable one. It is the spur that urges us onward when the way becomes hard, and thereby serves in our accomplishments. Acquisitiveness is a good motive stretched too far. It is a fine line that separates good from evil; on one side are love, good sportsmanship, and acceptance of our rewards, while on the evil side is an insistent *demand* for a reward.

"Me and mine" is a slogan of the devil greed. It is afraid—afraid its good will pass it by. If we fall into the mistaken belief that there is a limit to the supply of good, greed is at hand to take over our consciousness. It will slyly remind us that we have a right to the good things of life, and it will insinuate that others are taking our share. Once greed has occupied our consciousness, it settles in for a long stay and may color even our simplest activities.

Like the other devils, greed cannot withstand prayer and understanding. It melts like a dripping candle when the light of Truth comes upon it. One thing that annihilates greed is the realization that we need have no fear of a short supply of good. Our parts have been set aside, and there is abundance. Greed is unnecessary. It does no one any good but can do immeasurable harm. It stifles creativity, intensifies worry, loses friends, and can even make us ill.

Even so innocuous a thing as impatience can trigger greed into activity. The feeling that our goals are too long in coming can give rise to the worry that they will not come at all, or if they do come, they will be diminished. All this can cause an illumined mind to fall into fear and to invite greed.

Envy

Many of us contend with this adversary! Envy is mean, paltry, quibbling, base, and despicable. We know this, but let someone pass us by and reach a higher position, and the old devil envy begins to stir.

At first glance, envy may appear to be a mild, even insignificant condition, but it can swell into a conflagration that can consume us, a painful affliction of our confidence that can scar us for life. Do not underestimate this adversary. But likewise do not underestimate our defenses against it.

Envy cannot bear to look into the light. It is its undoing. When recognized, it is on its way out. Replace it with love and blessing for your neighbor. Know that what another can do you can do also, and greater things can you do. With this, envy is headed for oblivion.

The prayer of faith is a strengthening prayer. Meditation on the almightiness of Spirit within dispels fear, replaces despair with confidence, renews our courage and determination, and brings back the joy of perfect security in the eternal and unswerving love of God.

The devils would have us believe they are invincible. Do not believe it. They exist only in mind.

Hate

Hate is the boldest of the seven devils. There is nothing subtle or behind-the-scenes about it. It is out in front in all its ugliness, and it does not attempt to hide behind good intentions. The starkness of the emotion it typifies reveals it as an adversary for all to see and abhor.

One who is under the influence of hate is not a pretty person. Hate is violent, virulent. It sears one's soul and can lead to acts of irreparable wrongdoing. Far back in the genealogy of hate is the human sense of rightfulness. But hate has been allowed to grow from that small beginning and to become a devil.

Hate seldom springs full-blown into being. It matures at a measured pace and becomes more venomous at every stage. Near its beginning it probably occupied a milder form, perhaps dislike, which is a lesser demon and could quite easily have been obliterated in this weaker state. Dislike of a person or thing will fade with understanding and reason. It has a fragile foundation that tends to collapse at the application of knowledge; but when allowed to grow, it emerges into a tenacious adversary.

In any exercise in which hate plays a part, the hater is harmed more than the hated. All negation has a harmful effect on one's mind, body, and affairs. It warps one's judgment, crumbles the creative essence in one's soul, clouds one's thinking processes, weakens one's body against malfunctioning, and in fact, increases aberrant systems in one's mind and body functions. It even changes one's facial characteristics. This adversary is malevolent; it is a spoiler and a killjoy, a stumbling block, and an undercover obstructionist. It is a powerful enemy of our success and happiness. Get rid of it.

If we hate anyone or anything, we must

eliminate this adversary from our minds before it does immeasurable harm. We must not hate anything, not even evil; for of such stuff are fanatics made. Fanaticism is giving our minds to an unhealthy emotion that produces a distorted view.

We need to be constantly on guard against this adversary. Like all the others, it is devious, lurking in the outer darkness to take advantage of every opportunity. It will take a small thing, such as indignation over some wrong done to us or to society, or a simple dislike for a person or issue, and build it. It is a coward. Arrogant and brazen as it seems, it is no match for our wills. Say to it, as Jesus did: *"Begone, Satan!..."* (Matt. 4:10) and it will slink away. After all, it is nothing more than a false concept. Change your attitude, and hate fades into the mists of nothingness. Remember this: If this adversary has come into your mind, even though it has become firmly entrenched, your freedom is only a thought away.

The opposite of hate is love, and in any confrontation, love conquers. Jesus said: *"Love your enemies...."* (Luke 6:27) When you love your enemies, hate disappears. Love is the greatest power. Love is natural to you, whereas hate is foreign. Open your mind and heart, and love flows in smoothly, and devils and demons scatter before it.

Love your seeming enemies, love your friends, love your family, your city, and your country. Love is the greatest blessing you can give another and yourself. You do not have to condone the evil another does in order to love the evildoer. Love the good in him. Love the Christ in him, and you will bless both him and yourself. Hate cannot abide in love.

Fear

The fifth devil, fear, wears a coat of many colors.

Fear is perhaps the easiest devil to eliminate. Reasoning can single-handedly evaporate it. Fear is a volatile adversary; it comes and goes, swells and diminishes, and waxes robust or feeble in accordance with the degree of jeopardy ascribed to the situation.

In spite of its flightiness and unsubstantiality, fear is strong. Its effect is metamorphic. In an extreme state, it can transform a normally stable individual into a helpless one. Fear can freeze our minds, stiffen our muscles, dissolve our strength, enfeeble our resolve, and render us incapable of rational thought.

In a coat of another color it comes into the mind as indecision and uncertainty; it attacks self-confidence; it saps the will. It works against progress, against making friends, and against consideration of new and profitable ventures. In the form of timidity, it deadens personality.

The study of psychology tells us that the primary impulse when one is faced with sudden danger is "flight or fight." This is not all bad. Certainly there are times when it is desirable to flee from danger, either physically or in mind. When we face an attitude that we realize is dangerous to our well-being, it is right that we withdraw quickly to safer thinking. In a situation of physical danger, flight is not only natural but sensible. We have an obligation to preserve our bodies, our minds, and our moral structure against all dangers. We must be concerned about the beautiful person God has created, the masterpiece of self-perpetuating form in which we live. We have been given a precious possession in the amazing combination of cells that make up our physical brains and control our

thinking processes, and our perceptive qualities. It is our duty to protect our ideals from
inroads of ignoble motives, to protect our
capacity to exercise our talents from attacks
of lethargy and self-doubt, to protect our beliefs in our integrity and status from conditions that would demean and stifle us. But
these are in the category of flight, not fight—
taking flight back into the energizing, uplift-
ing, restorative mind of God through prayer.
Fleeing to the safety of proper concepts is
more often than not the best way to fight
dangerous problems. Flight or fight—these
are normal responses to peril that often are
expressed in the same way. Fight has a negative connotation. Let us translate it into mental resistance.

Reacting to the potential danger in evil or
error and withdrawing to a safer position is
not wrong. It is self-preservation. Shall we
say then that fear has good qualities? This is
the subtlety of it. When we speak of concern
or solicitude, we are not talking about the
devil fear. Fear is exaggeration, the wolf
masquerading as the lamb. Terror, dread,
consternation, and panic are other names for
this adversary. It can overwhelm us, distort
our reasoning, cause the breath to catch in

our throats, or make our hearts stop beating. In another and equally debilitating state, it is timidity, or weakness, or irresolution, any of which may suffocate our initiative and effectively work against the attainment of our potential capability.

Learn to recognize the difference between prudence and fear. Prudence is far from being synonymous with fear; rather, prudence is acting sensibly and in faith with due regard to our personal debt to creation. Prudence guards the divine purpose for which we were made.

Fear, along with the other adversaries, is the root of much seeming iniquity in the world. Left alone it may, through devious means, promote cheating, license, thievery, hopelessness, even murder. On occasion it may call its fellow adversaries—greed, hate, envy, and selfishness—to concentrate their evils upon us. It is a devil without substance, a force without rationale, but with far-reaching effects. The sooner we begin to extricate fear from our consciousness, the more quickly we will be free.

It may be difficult to overcome our fears. The baby's first fear is that of falling, then those around him begin to instill others. He learns all manner of apprehensions—fear of lightning, getting his feet wet, strangers, the "boogey" man, being naughty, anything out of the ordinary, the dark, the devil, mushrooms, spiders, snakes, and anything bigger than he is. Quite likely the child then proceeds to manufacture his own fears. Is it any wonder that fear has become so closely woven into the fabric of our being? It was instilled in us, and we have fed it well.

This adversary takes many forms other than that of physical fear. For example, fear of being laughed at and fear of failure inhibit our progress and are destructive to our self-esteem. They make us unable to express ourselves. They convince us that we had better not try for a better job; and they refuse to permit us to take a chance on a potentially profitable venture. They find a hundred ways to discourage us.

Franklin Delano Roosevelt said: *There is nothing to fear but fear itself,* which sounds good and may have been right for the time. But in essence, it doubles the consequence. Do not even fear fear. Put your reasoning mind to work to destroy the adversary.

Consider the senselessness of fear. One of my first jobs was as a salesman. I remember that on my first call I carried my sample case around the block three times before I worked up the courage to enter the store and approach the merchant. My days in the job were agony until I got rid of my fear. I finally asked myself, "After all, what can this merchant do to me? He's not going to hit me with a club or call the police. He probably is a nice fellow and is waiting right now to welcome me."

Fear is a devastating adversary. It creeps into every phase of our lives, dampening our effectiveness. It slows our progress, denies us freedom. Its sphere ranges from concern and anxiety to terror. It works stubbornly and effectively to produce its wicked works. But let us always remember that it is nothing. The only power it has it receives from us. It is constantly being defeated but never gives up until we deny it a place in our minds. When the Truth is known, we have nothing to fear.

Countless times we have seen evanescent fear vanish into oblivion. Situations have evolved to their conclusions and have revealed that beyond the dire appearance there was absolutely no threat to us. Fear, of course, cannot remain where there is no threat to be seen.

We can cure ourselves of recurring fear. We can stand free, forever joyous in the knowledge of our emancipation. We gain freedom from all problems, including fear, through the application of prayer. Pray, not *against* fear, but *for* understanding. Pray until you arrive at the realization that you abide in the exalted state of a son of God. Your inheritance is wisdom, strength, abundance, and protection. In this knowledge you are invincible.

Selfishness

Now let us take a look at the devil selfishness. It, too, is a sly one. Perhaps the less said about it the better. In fact, maybe none of the seven devils should be given the distinction of much exposure, except that they cannot stand the light. They shrink from the spotlight and strive to hide behind our excuses, clichés, and the habit of long acceptance. They are familiar fixtures in most households. Let us bring them all out on stage and watch them squirm, cower, and fade before our eyes. With the knowledge and strength we have gained from knowing their vulnerability, we dispatch them to our personal never-never land, and we never see them again.

Meanwhile, selfishness continues to make us unhappy, unpopular, and unbalanced. This adversary grows from the normal tendency of all living things to protect their own. Jesus said: *"... give, and it will be given to you..."* (Luke 6:38) *"the measure you give will be the measure you get."* (Matt. 7:2) Selfishness will permit us to give only grudgingly that which is required from us. This adversary says, "Hold on to what you have because someone might take it from you. Get as much of your neighbor's share as he will permit, because there is not enough to go around, and it is easier to get it from him than to battle the world." Selfishness is crafty; it induces us to think only of ourselves and our advantage at the expense of others, and thereby causes us to break the divine law of love.

You might ask, what harm can a little selfishness do? It seems a minor thing to include among the seven devils. Sometimes we are inclined to defend it, declaring that we have a right to hang on to what is ours, against which basic premise there is little argument. The adversary is the exaggeration.

Selfishness ranks high among the adversaries as a producer of inharmony, unpopularity, dissatisfaction, failure, lack, and sundry other evils, some of which seemingly have little to do with selfishness. They may culminate in serious problems, such as bankruptcy or a general breakdown of moral and physical fibers. The devil fear is a close partner to selfishness. Acquisitiveness is another name for this adversary, as are stinginess, miserliness, parsimony, money-grubbing, and meanness. Who would want names such as these used in connection with them? The very selfish person is called all of them. He suffers without realizing that he is the cause of his suffering. It is simple to cure—with a change of mind.

Selfishness works on the consciousness. It puts its stamp on our concepts of events and on that of our fellowmen, and distorts our approaches to life. It is grasping and small-minded, ascribing its penuriousness to others. It lives with the dislike, even contempt, of its neighbors, thereby missing much pleasure, profit, and personal fulfillment. But it is vulnerable to understanding.

How do we escape its clutching fingers? In the same manner that we eliminate all its brethren: by exposing it for the imposter it is. That is a sure cure. Understanding is all it takes; and understanding comes from meditation and the acceptance of love and guidance from God. The wisdom and perception of Divine Mind are at the foundation of our being, and they reveal to us the beautiful truth when we open our minds. The truth sometimes embarrasses us. A selfish attitude can mean that we are weak, that we fear for our security, that we envy our neighbor, that we have a poor self-image, or that we are lazy. It also means that we are falling short of our potential of both happiness and accomplishment.

Opposites of selfishness are generosity and benevolence. Cultivate these, and selfishness will diminish.

It is neither necessary nor advisable to pry into our consciousness or probe painfully into our minds to discover if selfishness is there; we will know it by its fruits.

One who realizes that selfishness holds a place in his makeup needs to find a new understanding of himself. He should look to his true nature. No one is born selfish, just as no one is born a criminal, a saint, a beggar, or a captain of industry. It all happens afterward. God, who has freely given us life, dominion, love, and unlimited potential, surely exhibits no selfishness; and we are of God. He has given Himself without stint. We cannot stretch our minds far enough to conceive of His largesse. He holds nothing of Himself from us.

"... *give, and it will be given to you; good measure, pressed down, shaken together, running over, will be put into your lap ...* " (Luke 6:38) Jesus said. That is a direct promise from Him. There is nothing in this promise to indicate that you are in danger of running short after you give; instead, He said, in order to receive, give. It naturally follows that to refrain from giving is to cheat ourselves. We block the flow. To give is the primary rule for abundance, as well as for general well-being.

This is not to infer that we should confine giving to money, or to any other single gift. Share in whatever way is needed. Give friendship, compassion, understanding. Above all, give love. Give freely, without demands. You will receive in like kind, multiplied.

Negativism

The seventh devil is negativism. It is skeptical, an objector. It not only will not act as requested, but deliberately goes the opposite way. It is together a prophet of doom and a perverse egotist. It is a killjoy, never permitting an encouraging word to go by without challenge. It also serves as a cover-up for the devil fear.

Negative persons, by spreading gloom like a blanket, are dispiriting to all who come into contact with them. But the most serious harm is done to themselves. It has been well established, to most people's satisfaction, that we attract our own good or evil by our general attitudes. Think about failure hard enough and long enough, and you will fail. Expect misfortune, and it will not disappoint you. Believe you are not as competent or as lucky as the next person, and he will surpass you, unless he also is a negativist (in which case you are in a dead heat). Express conviction that there will be a downpour the day of the picnic, and you will be the one who gets wet.

The negativist justifies his gloom by claiming that he has been right many times in the past. Even once is sufficient proof for him. It is inevitable that he will be right—the whole creative power of his mind is working on it. Of course nothing turns out right for him.

How can it? Why shouldn't he be the one who spills gravy on his vest at the dinner? He planned it that way—unknowingly—but he planned it.

Negativism is the heartbeat of the other six devils. Take him out of them and they will be something else, or perhaps nothing at all. Without knowing the specifics of a person's problem, you can safely diagnose that this adversary is at the bottom of it. You will be right nine times out of ten. When negativism enters our minds, it overwhelms us, and henceforth directs our thinking along its stultifying course. Negativism sabotages every effort. It is our primary adversary.

The opposite of negativism is affirmation. Both cannot remain in our thoughts at the same time. In any earnest confrontation, affirmation inevitably wins because it is our natural state of being. Negativism is wholly unnatural, an add on.

Affirm. Affirm the good. Affirm the good with all the joyous expectancy of your heart. Your joy will grow to exultation as you continue to affirm. Watch the good crowd into your life, pressed down, shaken together, running over. This is the cure for negativism. Have faith in the right outworking of every situation. Affirm good, and thank God that it is so. Take the positive view, and negativism will go headfirst out the window.

Now you have the whole sorry lineup of devils. Look at them briefly. Look at them and laugh: bombastic willfullness, rapacious greed, green-eyed envy, glowering hate, slavering fear, worry-wart selfishness, mournful negativism. Not a pretty ensemble, is it? Are these the kinds of guests you want to entertain in your life? Open the door and heave them out, one by one, for good.

What does all this have to do with prayer? Everything. What else but prayer can save you from the seven devils? The adversaries are overwhelming but unsubstantial, influential but insignificant, powerful yet have no power of their own. All yield to prayer. Denial and affirmation are fundamental in prayer. Deny the evil and affirm the good. Deny the seven devils and affirm their opposites—willingness, givingness, love, solicitude, faith, generosity, affirmation. Pray for release from the adversaries who inhibit your progress toward divinely potential accomplishment. They stultify. Do not put up with them. Thank God for the prayer of faith that releases you from all evil.

It is important to remember that prayer is concentrated and directed thought. Earnest thought must ultimately manifest in our lives and affairs. A prayer based on fear emphasizes that which we are afraid of, and it works in reverse. A prayer based on anger or envy or greed is not a prayer to God but an invitation to the adversaries to come back in. Let us pray always—in faith, joy, and love—a prayer that we can believe in our hearts is acceptable in God's sight.

Don't ever forget that the seven devils are not true adversaries. A landslide across the road might be considered an adversary to progress; it is real, substantial. The seven devils exist solely in our own heads. They are manufactured products—seconds, at that.

Let us sing a paean of gratitude to God that His greater power frees us permanently from seeming adversaries.

There are no devils—only illusions!

Father or Son?

Prayer means different things to different people. To one person it is earnest supplication that a desired good may come about. To another it is meditation on a spiritual idea without the need to make a specific request, but endeavoring to rise into a state of conscious at-one-ment with Divine Mind. Others feel that prayer is a reverent conversation with a higher power. Still others pray an affirmative prayer, affirming, as Jesus Christ did, that the ideal they desire is now manifested.

People pray in different ways at different times, depending on their needs. All forms of prayer, however, have at least one purpose in common—to associate oneself with a power greater than one's own and to partake of the blessings, spiritual or material, of that association. The form that a prayer takes is less important than the strength of faith in one's consciousness.

It is a phenomenon of the human condition that prayer is an integrating factor in life. Everyone prays in one form or another. But certain differences appear in the purposes and methods of prayer among races and creeds. In Christianity, for example, an important concept has aligned opposing forces in a continuing and sometimes bitter dispute: to whom should we pray—to God or to Jesus Christ?

Some will ask, what's the difference? True prayer, they insist, is love for and faith in Spirit within one's own heart, and the name one gives to Spirit is not important. When you earnestly pray a prayer of faith, it will surely find its place and produce the desired result. The result is primarily in the effect the prayer has on your own consciousness anyway. Let us always remember that in prayer we are not trying to influence God, or Jesus, or anyone else to change His mind about our needs. We pray to change ourselves, to open our minds for the inflow of the good we seek.

Some believe that the resurrected Jesus is closer to humanity than God is, and that He understands the problems of people after having met the same problems. But many persons feel more comfortable and confident praying to the Father, whom they look upon as the authority figure. Still others believe that God and Jesus are one—that God came bodily to Earth and took the form of Jesus Christ. This discussion has been going on for a very long time.

An Equal Ruling

At one point during the last century, the matter grew so serious that it portended grave consequences among the churches. People were asking questions, and the clergy was providing varying answers. The credibility of the clergy was deterioriating. As a result, a conclave of representatives of divergent fundamentalist churches came together and spent many days in far-ranging and sometimes heated discussion. At last they hammered out a statement for publication, to which all did not fully subscribe but which represented the best possible compromise. Their conclusion was that God and Jesus are equal, full partners in running the universe. Both are divine, they declared. Both are Godlike and equally worthy of hearing prayers. The discussion continues. Father or Son? Evangelists continue to exhort their listeners to "come to Jesus!" A born-again Christian is taken to be one who has accepted Jesus as his personal Lord.

There remains a very fine line between the deity of God and of Jesus Christ. Most Christians accept Jesus Christ as the Savior of humankind, but some go far beyond that. Some students of religious tradition have concluded that religion was in a bad way at the time of Jesus. Man had strayed far from God. The law of Moses had lost its urgency and, in both public and private life, people gave evidence of denying their religious heritage. Jesus came and, by His example and teaching, led the way back to God.

Jesus was clearly a man who walked the Earth and, except for a notable excitement at the manner of His birth, grew to manhood under somewhat the same circumstances as other boys of His time. But Jesus was quite different from the others. The little that is known of His life reveals that He grew at a different spiritual pace than His comrades. When He was twelve years old, He confounded the priests at the temple with His

understanding. When chided by His mother
for not remaining close beside her and
Joseph, He said: "... *I must be in my
Father's house.*" (Luke 2:49) Yet He became a
carpenter, and remained so until He was
thirty years old. We know that He grew into
the ideal Man of God, gaining an infinitely
greater understanding of the divinity within
Himself than that attained by any other person. He performed miracles of healing. He
demonstrated authority over His own mind
and body, and over all forms of matter everywhere. He recognized that the power and
dominion He demonstrated many times in
His life, as in His miracles, came directly to
Him from God. But He did not claim to be
God, except insofar as all people are gods. On
the contrary, He said: "... *he who believes in
me will also do the works that I do; and
greater works than these will he do....*"
(John 14:12) The multitudes to whom He
preached did not understand Him, nor did
His followers or His disciples. They thought
He had come to establish a kingdom on Earth
to rescue the Jews from the oppression of
Rome and from tyrants in other lands.

Jesus had come instead as a Way-Shower,
as a manifestation of the divinity in man,

which comprises all the qualities and powers of Father God.

He Became the Christ

No one knows through what means Jesus attained the divine stature of the ideal Man, which is complete oneness with God. He was born Jesus of Nazareth, and He became Jesus the Christ. Christ is the creative word of God, the divine essence in every man and woman. Christ is the divinity, the life, the potential within us. Christ is the I AM, the perfect idea of God in us. Christ is the Son of God, and, likewise, the Daughter of God. You are Jesus Christ in training. Only Jesus fulfilled His potential and emerged as God-Man, demonstrating in full measure the miracle-working power of God that manifests as the Christ.

The Lord referred to in Scripture is the Christ. "*. . . for to you is born this day in the city of David a Savior, who is Christ the Lord.*" (Luke 2:11) When we pray to the Lord, we are praying to the Christ which is the divine idea manifested. The Christ is the gift of God, the gift of Himself to all His children. God is all in all. Christ is in all, because Christ is of God. No child was ever born without the Christ Presence, and no man or woman can ever grow old enough to outgrow the Christ. Every moment of every day, the I AM (Christ) is our unfailing Lord within, sent to us by the Father as our divine life essence, our strength, our dominion, and our wisdom. Frederick William Henry Meyers, a poet of the last century, summed it up this way: *Christ is the end, for Christ is the beginning, Christ the beginning for the end is Christ.*

The realization that our personal, ever-present Christ is the Son of the Most High, eternally abiding within us as our spiritual identity and having direct contact with God, is cause for great rejoicing. It is also cause for sober reflection on the responsibilities of our sonship.

Let us examine the words of Jesus Christ to learn the concept of His relationship with God. He said: *"Not everyone who says to me, 'Lord, Lord,' shall enter the kingdom of heaven, but he who does the will of my Father who is in heaven."* (Matt. 7:21) When the disciples asked Him for instruction in prayer, He gave them the Lord's Prayer, which begins: *"Our Father ... "* He also said: *"And call no man your father on earth, for you have one Father, who is in heaven.*" (Matt. 23:9) Also, "*When you have lifted up the Son of man, then you will know that I am he, and that I do nothing on my own authority but speak thus as the Father taught me.*" (John 8:28) John 15:10 records Jesus' promise: "*If you keep my commandments, you will abide in my love, just as I have kept my Father's commandments and abide in his love.*" Later, in John 16:28 we read: "*I came from the Father and have come into the world; again, I am leaving the world and going to the Father.*"

When we pray in the name of Jesus Christ, we are praying in the nature, or consciousness, of Jesus Christ. This is the consciousness of divine realization, a sure knowing that our prayers are answered as His prayers were answered. Praying in the nature of Jesus Christ means that we lift our consciousness to at-one-ment with God, and in this state our prayers are inevitably answered in the same terms as our requests. We are in the same room with God, speaking His language in direct conversation. This will bring quick manifestation of our desires.

No one has seen God, but many persons declare that Jesus Christ has appeared to them in times of stress or need. God is Principle, not flesh. Jesus Christ is the manifested Son, the demonstration of humanity's spiritual identity. I have never seen Jesus Christ, but some insist that He has appeared to them clearly in semi-material form, always as the Comforter when they most needed Him. Some will scoff at the thought of Jesus coming forth out of invisibility and appearing to certain individuals. But who can gainsay persons who report divine visitations with such confidence and earnestness? His appearance, the disbelievers might explain, was no doubt a dream or a hallucination. None can prove that He has materialized in their sight, although He promised that He, the manifestation of the Christ self in every person, would appear. In John 15:26, Jesus said: *"But when the Counselor comes, whom I shall send to you from the Father, even the Spirit of truth, who proceeds from the Father, he will bear witness to me...."* However, it makes little difference, except perhaps to a scholar, whether Jesus actually came forth to be seen by persons in their time of need, or whether in moments of high spiritual consciousness His image was impinged upon their minds. The result is the same.

To whom then should we pray—to God the Father, or to Jesus the Son? In John 16:23-24, Jesus told His disciples: *"Truly, truly, I say to you, if you ask anything of the Father, He will give it to you in my name. Hitherto you have asked nothing in my name; ask, and you will receive, that your joy may be full."* God is our Father, Jesus our Brother. Our Brother demonstrated the high potential of our Christhood. He performed the healing, prospering, harmonizing work of God, revealing to all humankind the work we are divinely equipped and charged to do.

Many persons yearn for a personal God with whom they can identify. God as principle or law seems cold and distant, an august and uncompromising lawgiver, by whose stern judgment we are acquitted or condemned. But when we think of Him as love, total love, a divine being, whose great love is poured upon His children without measure, our concept of Him will soften. Thinking of God as Principle, unless we discover what divine Principle is, may lead us into misconceptions of our relationship to Him. Principle is Law; it is fundamental Truth; it is the spiritual integrity of God, and comprises all that God is, which is without limit, wholly immeasurable. Principle is without weight or form, yet it is the divine activity by which all is formed. Let us always hold in mind the truth that God exists, though not in flesh; He is Spirit. He is not emotionally human as we are, but divine, and out of Him we become human. He accompanied us to this plane as the divine Essence within, our I Am.

He Guides Us

God walks beside us, but we do not see Him; we may not even realize He is there, except perhaps in a moment of peril when He snatches us from danger. Nevertheless, He guides us if we but listen.

Although He does not greet us each morning in language we can understand, He is personal to us. He is our love, our joy, our health, and our fulfillment. He is our potential, our intelligence, and our dominion over the affairs of our lives. No blessing ever came to us that He did not send. No misfortune ever gets past His protecting arms, unless we deny Him and invite it in. He hears every prayer, and He never says no. Only through His love and power can we manifest the desires of our hearts.

To some this is not enough. We want to talk things over. We feel the need for someone to guide our steps, to pick us up when we fall. We ask for someone to sympathize with our hurts, to urge us onward when the going is hard, to serve as a silent but contributing partner in our affairs. God is all these, but we do not always understand His language.

Go Within

If you would talk things over, go within. If you need reassurance, go within. If you have lost your way and need guidance, go within. Go within to your I AM, the spiritual you, the Son of God or Christ presence. The I AM is your God-self, your place in Truth and Spirit. Nothing can be closer than your I AM, which comprises all the qualities of God bound up in the Christ within.

The Christ is you in your inner realm. Jesus Christ is the perfect expression of the Son of God. In Him the Christ came forth into perfect human form as it was always meant to do for each of us. Jesus elevated His consciousness until He was one with God in Mind, and He performed the healing, prospering, and authoritative work of God on Earth. This also is your destiny. If you need companionship, talk to the Christ in your heart. He is the love of God, who loves you more than anyone else can. He will lead you, direct you, reassure you, but only when you lift your eyes to the serenity of Divine Mind in which He abides.

To whom should you pray? Pray to God, with Jesus Christ as your Teacher. Pray as Jesus told you to pray. Pray the Lord's Prayer, and in the same vein make your wants known to Him. Jesus prayed to our Father and performed miracles of healing and blessing. He said that whatever we ask of God in His consciousness, we will receive, in His consciousness, His nature. Pray as Jesus prayed. You will never find a better model to follow. Pray in Jesus' name, and you will lift yourself into perfect freedom on Earth.

If You Can!

A certain man, with a son who had been afflicted with violent seizures since childhood, appeared before Jesus. The man pleaded: "... *it has often cast him into the fire and into the water, to destroy him; but if you can do anything, have pity on us and help us.*" *And Jesus said to him, "If you can! All things are possible to him who believes.*" (Mark 9:22, 23) Jesus rebuked the unclean spirit and it came out, and the boy was healed.

Later, the disciples asked Jesus privately: ... "*Why could we not cast it out?*" *And He said to them, "This kind cannot be driven out by anything but prayer.*" (Mark 9:28, 29)

"*If you can!*" He said. "*All things are possible to him who believes.*" Think carefully about these words, for in them is contained the formula you have been seeking—the formula for answered prayer.

Let us say that you have a problem, and you pray earnestly for its solution. You believe implicitly in the problem, but do you believe in the solution? All things are possible to you if you believe, Jesus said. Conversely, it would be true that nothing is possible to you if you do *not* believe. If our approach to prayer is made up of one-half belief, one-fourth belief, two-thirds belief, or some other fraction of total belief, the results will show it.

We pray constantly, even when we do not realize it. Every small desire is a prayer. Our prayers are always being answered. But they may be only partially answered—one-half, one-third, one-tenth. They may seem rarely to be answered fully. Why? Because we have not prayed in total faith, in unassailable belief that our prayers will be answered totally. When you pray, remind yourself that Jesus said that if you believe, all things are possible to you.

Throughout the Gospels, Jesus spoke of the efficacy of faith: "... *your faith has made you well,*" (Matt. 9:22; Mark 5:34;

10:52; Luke 8:48) *"Your faith has saved you,"* (Luke 7:50) *"According to your faith be it done to you."* (Matt. 9:29) He also said, *"And whatever you ask in prayer, you will receive, if you have faith."* (Matt. 21:22) He promised repeatedly that healing, prosperity, and complete salvation are ours, but we must believe.

The Faith of Jesus Christ

How frequently do we pray with unquestioning expectation? Jesus Christ had faith in God. He knew His prayers would be answered. He was so certain that He risked the ridicule of onlookers when He publicly called forth Lazarus from death. Many times He healed sickness and deformity in the presence of great crowds. He changed water into wine at a party and fed a multitude with a few fish and loaves of bread. Would we be so bold? Perhaps our faith reaches just so far as to assure our accumulating sufficient funds for our next car payment, but would we ever expect enough money to pay off the entire loan? Jesus felt no such limitation; He knew the extent of His accomplishment was limited only by His own expectation. We need to work toward the same realization.

Some people hold their expectations low so they will not be disappointed or embarrassed if they fail. Other people hesitate to ask God because they feel it would be presumptuous. They believe they are not worthy or important enough. There are others who categorize prayer. An ordinary need they will readily pray for, but anything that seems beyond the ordinary frightens them.

Every answered prayer, large or small, is a miracle. And if we are to be free to pray effectively, we must be open to expectation of miracles.

Perhaps we need to change our thoughts about ourselves. Some of us look upon ourselves as insignificant in the sight of God. Perhaps we know ourselves and our imperfections too well, and we dwell on this uncomfortable knowledge. Some of us may believe that no one with an imperfection has a right to expect preferential treatment, such as a miracle. What such people need is a sure knowledge that they are close to God, children of God. And regardless of past mistakes, they are divine beings. By its very nature a divine being cannot be weak, inept, or unworthy.

Do you find it easier to believe in miracles

for someone else? Do other people always seem more assured, infinitely more competent, a lot luckier, more worthy of success and other blessings of God? Do you look at other persons, whom you consider to have achieved success in one form or another, and see revealed in them a great many "no-nos" with respect to ideals you have considered essential to a good life? Perhaps you see them as ruthless, or aggressive, unloving, or insensitive to others' needs. Yet, you feel they are successful. Why, you may ask, can't such miracles happen to me?

True Success

I once knew a man who had what most people would love to possess—riches, security, position, and a way of life that included all that money could buy. But he was anything but an object of envy. One could only sympathize with him. He had an enormous capacity for acquiring wealth, but he also had a mind riddled by fear, he was a hypochondriac, and he had a vastly distrustful nature. Was he truly successful?

Jesus said: *"If you can! All things are possible to him who believes."* Perhaps some of us have taken His statement to mean only that all things are possible to him who believes in God or Jesus Christ. This most certainly is true, but let us take the liberty for a moment of adding to the quotation so that it reads: All things are possible to him who believes he can have them, or accomplish them, or is worthy of them.

Would you believe that a lanky youth with little education, chopping wood outside his parents' log cabin in Illinois, could aspire to the office of President of the United States? Abraham Lincoln did. Would you believe that a penniless immigrant behind a pushcart on the streets of New York, peddling cookies his wife had baked, could dream of becoming one of the world's richest men? John Jacob Astor did. The annals of business, science, the arts, and politics are replete with examples of men and women with beginnings of poverty, repression, and other such disadvantages who achieved high success. Would you say that such people revealed a good self-image, that each believed he was worthy? Each obviously considered himself capable of attaining his long-held dream. Jesus Christ was not born of wealthy parents, neither was His way made easy by friends in high places, but you know what He accomplished. He believed in God, and He believed in Himself.

The Self-Image Factor

Improve your self-image, and you automatically improve the quality of your life. A good self-image gives us assurance, faith in ourselves, and good personalities. A good personality is important in contacts with other persons. It is the face we show the world. It may be quite different from our individuality, which is the real you or me in a spiritual sense. Our individuality is our specific manifestation of God. It is unchanging. It is true and perfect. It is our personal God-self, and identifies us in spirit as personality identifies us in the world.

Your personality is what you have made out of your individuality by your interpretation of it. Your personality can, and does, change. You project a certain image at your place of employment, another at your home, another with your friends, and probably another when you are interviewing for a job.

While all these images are different to a degree, they have at least one factor in common—your conception of yourself. It is

apparent wherever you are and with whom-
ever you speak. You are identified by your
self-image—assured, happy, fearful, confident, morose, surly, or whatever else may be
your habitual attitude.

We form habits of personality. If we com-
monly think of ourselves as second-rate, we
will assume that kind of personality. And,
although we may assume a forced outer self
in response to a particular situation, we
quickly resume our habitual image when the
situation has passed.

If we consider ourselves of little consequence in the world, less capable than others,
we cannot escape being inhibited, self-depre-
cating, and usually unadventurous. Inhibition is not only an enemy of a pleasing personality but also of progress, because it re-
strains us from expressing the capable and
likeable persons we really are. While it is important that we recognize and profit from our
mistakes, excessive preoccupation with them
can result in more inhibition that can produce
hesitation to do anything for fear of blunder-
ing. Self-criticism has its place, but too much
can deaden our approach to any undertaking
and cause us to become unproductive.

It all begins in the mind. Success mechanisms, self-image, and joy and fulfillment are born in our thinking processes, and so are our failures. It is impossible to work effectively toward a goal unless we believe in our hearts that we possess the qualifications needed to attain it and to enjoy it. Our success mechanisms and our failure mechanisms are inextricably entwined with our self-images.

If you are not satisfied with your accomplishments to date, consider your self-image. How do you appear to yourself? In what light do you view your talents, or seeming lack of them, your ability or inability to make friends easily, your past record of success or failure in manifesting your desires? Investigate your true, unvarnished, private opinion of yourself—not what you think you should think of yourself but what you *really* think of yourself. Can you tell yourself with full belief that you are capable, charming, successful, happy, or smart? If some of your answers are negative, do not impress the negation on your mind. Your self-criticism may be too harsh. Some of us tend to overemphasize our shortcomings in order to make sure we are not duped by our own minds. This, too, is the result of a poor self-image. In any event, deny the negative and affirm the positive, because only the positive is true.

It is natural for the mind to set goals. In whatever station in life we find ourselves, we have objectives, and we are either consciously satisfied or dissatisfied with our degree of attainment. We are never neutral about it. Our minds are equipped to develop proper and satisfying goals. Through a multitude of impressions and experiences, our thoughts form into trends of activity that develop patterns of desire. Regardless of the nature of our desires, we do or do not attain them in accordance with our self-evaluation.

I Can!

It is a cliché nowadays to declare that anything you think you can do, you can do, but it is an indisputable truth. It is a matter of faith in yourself and belief in your capabilities.

How does one build a good self-image? First we must believe that it is possible. We will need to change our thinking about ourselves, break long established habits of thought, and develop new and unaccustomed attitudes. We begin with the indisputable truth that we are beloved, capable children of God. God made no misfits, no natural failures. Every person arrived on this plane with a full complement of equipment needed to become successful and happy in his own way, whatever his station is to be. The basic equipment needs only to be organized and developed. We have the creativity of God, the wisdom of Divine Mind, to draw upon and use. We are born with intelligence, a natural aptitude, and an urge to utilize both to our full potential. Having faith in ourselves is a matter of believing in the divine spark within, which is the Christ. With all this going for us, what can be against us?

We all need to practice dominion over the affairs of our lives, to experience the thrill of knowing we can achieve our desires. In this regard, remember that the subconscious mind absorbs whatever messages we send it. It does not pause to analyze the message or to decide whether it is true or false. In fact, it neither knows nor cares whether it is true—it simply takes what we send and incorporates it as part of itself. This is how false notions become habitual attitudes through the action of the subconscious mind. The superconscious mind takes its inspiration from Spirit, the conscious mind absorbs leadings from our senses, the subconscious mind is influenced by both; and it is the preponderance on one side or the other that determines the trend of our attitudes. We are what we think.

If the subconscious mind does not differentiate between truth and falsehood, it does not know whether input from the conscious mind is from a true experience or a product of imagination. Therefore, we can repetitively imagine ourselves in any situation we desire, and the effect on our habit-forming mechanisms will be the same as if we actually experienced the situation or condition. Tests have been conducted by eminent scientists in which two basketball teams were the subjects. One team practiced shooting baskets assiduously every day for twelve weeks, while the other team gathered in a room and imagined themselves shooting baskets with fine precision. Neither team knew what the other was doing. At the end of the test, the teams competed with one another. It turned out that neither team gained a greater proficiency than the other, indicating the equal effectiveness of imagination and experience.

The subconsciousness is not a separate mind but a phase of our one mind, and it is an integral part of the thinking process. It does not originate thought. It accepts and stores information we give it and feeds it back to us on demand. It works all the time. It may push into the conscious mind the name of an acquaintance whom we haven't seen in years. When we request it to do so, it also sorts out and combines into an appropriate package impressions we have given it. It may wake us in the middle of the night to provide an answer to a problem we have been worrying about for a week.

Habit Formation

We form habits by holding the same thoughts consistently for a period of time, and whether those thoughts are true or false makes no difference in the process of habit formation. If we consistently think thoughts of failure, we will probably fail. If we think thoughts of success, we no doubt will succeed; we will be led and urged to follow whatever course is needed to achieve the success we envision. Forming habits of success-thinking will lead our minds to the conviction that our ambitions are possible.

As habits are formed, so can they be changed. Affirming Truth statements is effective in prayer even if those statements do not appear to be presently factual. If we accept them as statements of Truth, they will become interwoven into our consciousness and ultimately become a part of our habit mechanisms. Every habit is an executive part of us, directing our thinking and behavior in accordance with its own nature. We will follow it as long as it is in charge. We can escape it only by substituting a different trend of thought.

Affirming: *The love of God expresses through me* may engender a sense of guilt when we know in our hearts that we are not expressing love toward an individual. But, if we continue the affirmation, knowing that God's love is strong within us, we will form the habit of loving. Saying: *I am abundantly prospered* or *I am healed* in a critical situation of lack or illness may seem almost laughable. How can simply claiming prosperity make us prosperous in the face of great lack? Repeating words of faith draws them into consciousness where they take their place in our habitual attitudes. That which is true in consciousness becomes true in outer affairs. Miracles occur under such circumstances. Truth affirmations are good and effective builders of a good self-image.

We are meant to be successful, healthy, happy, and prosperous. If you have formed the habit of criticizing yourself, change the habit. Your own criticism can tear down your self-image faster and more completely than criticism from another. Your conscious self yearns for your approval and is devastated by your criticism. Approve of yourself. So you have made a mistake. So what? Everybody does. You need not blame yourself forever. Simply profit from the mistake. God loves and approves of you. Who are you to say He is wrong?

God does not love one person more than another; we are equal in His sight. Some receive more because they are able to accept more. A good self-image, belief in self, and approval of self, are prime requisites for opening the door to let the good pour in.

Do you have a great and unfulfilled desire? Believe! Believe, and know that it is yours. Know that it is now manifest, and proceed as though it were a fact in your life. Act as you expect to act when you receive it. Do not pray for God to give you your desire—He already has. Pray to convince yourself that it is yours.

If you think this is too simplistic to be true,

prove it. Hold in mind your highest goal. Love it, believe in it, believe that you are worthy of it, that you are equal to its demands, that it is good for you and others. Dispel every doubt and fear from your mind. Arrive at complete faith in God, in your goal, in yourself—then watch the miracles happen to and through you.

Prayer is the tried and proved way to your objectives, but you have a responsibility to prepare yourself. Prepare your mind and consciousness to receive.

Teach Us to Pray

Jesus prayed with His disciples and, when He was finished, one disciple said to Him: ... *"Lord, teach us to pray...."* (Luke 11:1) Jesus responded with the best-known prayer of all time, the Lord's Prayer. He began, *"Our Father...,"* and with these words He set the tone of His teaching. With *"Our Father"* He gathered together all of humankind into a common all-inclusive congregation and set before us one Being, Father of all. Jesus claimed Him as Father, *our* Father. Jesus spoke of His Father, the Father of His disciples, and of all people of the Earth down through the years; and today you and I may claim that He is our Father. He is our personal Father as well as the Father of all. It is well that we return to this realization frequently. What a comfort to know that we are children of the Most High and, though we may be prodigal sons, He plays no favorites.

This is our contact with God—Father to child; and this intimate relationship gives us the right to call upon Him for guidance, for encouragement, for the specific kind of help that satisfies each need.

When we pray to God, our Father, we touch the source of our inspiration as well as the source of our good. He gives both to us freely—inspiration to guide us into the appropriate pattern of expression that leads to our inheritance, and the ultimate good that is ours by divine right.

We pray to God, our Father, not for the purpose of appeasing Him, not to influence Him, not to cajole Him, not to demand of Him, but to align ourselves with His divine purpose in our lives. He has already given us all we will ever need to fulfill our potential and to continue in the academy of Spirit until we become as Jesus was, one with Him, which is the final goal of humankind.

Meanwhile, we pray for the fulfillment of our needs and desires with full confidence that our Father hears us and will respond. It is our faith in Him that impels us to release our fears and doubts and to open our minds to the free flow of His good into our affairs. Our good comes through our minds. This is where we accept our good, and our acceptance opens the door that was hitherto closed. When we sit in meditation or prayer, do we truly realize the enormous force we are touching and how fortunate we are that it works for us rather than against us? If you were asked to think of the greatest force you can conceive of, you might think of the hydrogen bomb, or perhaps the ocean, an even greater force. Fifty years ago you might have said the greatest force is a tornado, dynamite, an avalanche, a hurricane, or a volcano. What will you say 100 years from now after scientists have had time to develop bigger bombs, more complex and efficient fission and fusion of matter, or perhaps an esoteric and inscrutable force of power not dreamed of today? These concepts are not altogether reassuring, but they are a tabulation of man's frenetic preoccupation with devising ever greater sources of power. Beyond these symbols of power and beyond anything that will ever be devised by man is the awesome force of gravity.

Above all these, however, above all possible

mechanical, physical, and natural forces is the unparalleled power of God. There can be no greater power than God, because God is Power itself. The purest and most abundant energy is contained in Spirit. It is the energy that passes understanding, even comprehension. It performs miracles with spectacular ease; it cannot be defeated or even turned. Nothing is impossible to the power of God.

Divine power is gentle enough to heal a baby, great enough to stay the wind and flood and to perform miracles of transformation for all who believe. Your current problem is not too great for a power such as this. When you consider your need, it is miniscule compared to the power available to you. Alfred Lord Tennyson, in "Idylls of the King," wrote: *More things are wrought by prayer than this world dreams of.*

With this all-encompassing power at our call through prayer, is it any wonder that for thousands of years people have cried, "Teach us to pray?" A mystique has developed regarding prayer, and to many people it has become an esoteric ceremony that only ministers, priests, and rabbis are qualified to conduct. This is a pity. Prayer is a personal contact with God, a do-it-yourself thing. Other persons can pray with you, and their prayers can be effective in bolstering your own, but the greatest service another person can do for you is to instill faith in your consciousness that your personal prayer can and will be answered. Silent Unity receives hundreds of thousands of prayer requests, and countless persons are blessed with healing, prosperity, and harmonious conditions. Silent Unity tells of innumerable instances in which persons who have requested prayers by mail report they have received divine answers in their bodies, minds, and affairs immediately after mailing their request, before Silent Unity could have received it.

Prayer of Faith

They have tuned into the great spiritual aura surrounding Silent Unity, but chiefly they have experienced release from worried tension and have experienced an insurge of faith in their own hearts. Other religious organizations also have prayer centers to which people appeal for help and which report remarkable records of answered prayer. Their approach to God is sometimes quite different from Unity's, which seems to prove that God finds all prayers acceptable. God does not outline the form that prayer must take, but He asks only faith. The prayer of faith is the one that you can believe. Speaking from the level of understanding that He is not only omnipotent, omniscient, and omnipresent, but also the Source of love and compassion, one cannot conceive that God would demand that all His creations must approach Him with pleas for forgiveness for their sins, including having been born. Nor does He demand any kind of formalized prayer.

Rather, I expect Him to regard me as His beloved son, which I am through the Christ within, and to love me and approve of me, which I am convinced He does. It is His nature to forgive my sins before I commit them. I believe that my part is to express Him in all my ways, working to draw ever closer to the ideal He created in me in the beginning.

God is eternally urging us to receive from His abundant store of blessings in order to fulfill His purpose in our creation. Yet, many of us plead with Him to give us our desires, and we sometimes are astonished when He does. If you were scheduled for an interview for a fine new position and you learned that your prospective employer was not only willing but eager to hire you, you likely would approach him with assurance and confidence rather than imploring. When you pray, you outline the blessings you are ready to receive. God has told you in advance the blessings you desire are yours and has offered them to you freely and with love. It was He who specified the blessings. He awaits your call by placing strong desires in your heart. With perfect assurance that your prayer is already answered in Divine Mind and all that remains is your acceptance, state your claim in faith.

Your attitude of prayer needs to be transformed from doubt to thanksgiving and faith. You do not fear that God will not answer your prayer when you know that your fulfillment is even now in His outstretched hands.

Eliminate from your mind the fear that you are presumptuous in asking God for your deep desires. Do not consider that you are unworthy and unimportant, or that your request is too farfetched. Nothing God tells you to do can be considered farfetched. You can be sure that a strong hunch to take a specific positive action is God's instruction. You have a work to do in your corner of the world, and that work includes not only your personal health, well-being, and happiness, but also your contribution to the affairs of your environment and to the good of other persons. God is your perfect guide and counselor. He directs you, through your intuitive nature, into the paths that will speed you to your divine potential. You were born a divine being with Christ, the perfect Son of God, an integral part of your being. Perhaps unknowingly you blundered into divergent paths that drew you far from the pure dedication of your spiritual origin. God speaks to you in ... *a still small voice* (I Kings 19:12) and, whether or not you are aware of it, you are trying to reclaim your sonship. You have always experienced a sense of guilt when you missed the mark. You have probably called it your conscience bothering you. Long ago God set up a target in your consciousness as your spiritual guide.

God Is with You

When you pray, always remember that God is on your side. You are asking for what He told you He wants to give you. Follow His leading to your high ambitions; act on your hunches, for this is His guiding voice within. Neither doleful piety nor loud declamations or religiosity signify the true follower of Jesus Christ. The faith to accept His promises fully and a dedication to live His life of service after Him are proof of the effort to perfect one's mind, body, and affairs in accordance with the will of God.

The general prayer that seeks divine illumination and understanding of God's will is a fine and beautiful prayer, but it is not all that prayer is. On this plane of life we must deal with specifics, and specific prayer is the way. God has always dealt with specifics; He called for light, and there was light; He separated the light from the darkness; and He created the beasts of the field and the green things to feed them. He created the fishes and the sea for them to live in; and He created humankind. Nothing can be more specific than humankind with all its talents, moods, capacities, and complex structure. We have specific needs that God is prepared to supply. If we interpret prayer as a means of opening our minds to receive, we need specific as well as general prayers. Pray for your health; also pray for the headache that is bothering you. Pray for abundant prosperity; but do not neglect to pray for funds to pay the specific bill that soon will be due. Pray for harmony in your affairs; also pray to heal the immediate dissension between you and your brother. You need specific prayers so that you may focus on the solution at hand and gain assurance of release.

Pray to improve your consciousness, your attitude, your faith in God, but do not hesitate to ask for specific gifts. Some people feel it is mercenary to ask God to give them money to pay a bill or to heal a cold. But the specific need came from a specific cause which requires healing. The general prayer for understanding may not cause our minds to focus on the specific cause, and it will go unheeded. Complete understanding of the nature of God will heal all ills of the flesh and all errors of the mind. But until we attain to the beatific state of full understanding, let us not be afraid to pray for specific needs.

It is fine to pray for another, but first pray for yourself—not because your need is more important than the other person's, but because you need to prepare your mind and heart. You must develop faith, assurance, and love, and the conviction that what you ask for is the will of God. Never pray that another person will be made to change his mind or his ways in accordance with the way you think he ought to do or be. No matter how well you may know him, you do not know him well enough to decide what is best for him. Instead, place him in the loving hands of God, and pray that he will become open to the voice of intuition. This is why we need to pray for ourselves, to become able to release our loved one into the care of the One who is infinitely more capable than we.

This is a most difficult course to take. We are always sure we know how wrong the other person is and what he must do to get on the right track. While God is great, good, and powerful, we do not trust Him to know all the misguided things our loved one does. In a situation of intense interest, we move into the concept that God is limited and cannot be expected to know all that is going on. We must remember that God does not have to be told of our failings. Jesus Christ in us and in the other person is our guide and counselor and will direct our steps into the pleasant path that leads us both to our highest good. Spirit knows our needs and the needs of those for whom we pray, and what to do about both.

The best prayer for another is to see him surrounded by God's love, wisdom, healing, and protection. If the other person knows you are praying for him, the act of praying will increase his faith and thereby hasten the consummation. But do not tell God what to do for another person; He already knows. If the other person knows the nature of your request, it may distort his consciousness and bar the voice of God from coming through. Your part is to know that the one you pray for will be illumined for his highest good. The intercessory prayer can be effectual, benefiting both him who prays and him who is prayed for. Jesus Christ frequently prayed the intercessory prayer in addition to praying for Himself. He prayed for His disciples, and for *"them that believe on me."* His prayers reach even to this day and bind us to Him in bonds of love and faith. We pray for ourselves, our loved ones, and for the world, always remembering that we see with limited and personal view and there may be much more for us than we ask or can presently conceive. Let us pray for our desired manifestation without limiting it to that alone. As Unity minister and author Ernest Wilson frequently ended his prayers, "Lord, give me this or what in Thy sight is better."

Prayer is communion with God in which we ask in gratitude and faith for His blessings and listen for His response. Our faith is strong when it is based on the certainty that He never says no. Only we say no through our present inability to open our minds to accept. Instead of sitting at the feet of the teacher and begging, "Teach me to pray," we should stand before Him and say, "Teach me to accept." Training oneself to receive is the complex part. If you would receive a thing, you must first ask, and know that you ask, whether your request is a direct claim or a strong desire to receive. A desire in one's heart is an asking prayer, but if we view the desire as beyond our reach, it will remain so.

Daydreams are like this. Daydreams are in the nature of prayer, but usually they are simply pleasant notions of things that would be fun to have or to be, or delightful situations of self-indulgence that we enjoy reveling in but are too fanciful to be possible of manifestation. As such they serve no practical purpose. The only advantage in daydreams is that oftentimes our true potential is timorously hidden in them, and by repetition, our potential may come closer and at last appear less fanciful and show greater possibility. Prayers manifest from the inside-out, rather than from the outside-in. Answers to prayer come to you when you have developed the consciousness for them, and not before.

If this is true, we need to identify consciousness. Concisely, consciousness is our habitual attitude. It is the sum total of all the notions and beliefs acquired from past experiences and prior thinking that have settled into a definitely formed body of thought relating to anything that is in our present experience. It is our conception of things. Because it is our habitual pattern of thinking, our consciousness manifests itself in our lives and affairs. If we have a consciousness of health, that is, if we believe in health and fully expect it to remain in our bodies, we are healthy. If we have a consciousness of prosperity, we are prosperous. If we have a consciousness of peace, we are not easily disturbed. On the other hand, if we have a consciousness of limitation, it is bound to hold us in a state of lack. If we have a bad cold and we expect it to last two weeks, it will last that long, because that is our consciousness. If we are in a consciousness of health, we do not catch a cold.

In Unity we often hear, *all is consciousness.* This refers to the demonstrated truth that whatever your consciousness is, that is what you manifest. And you do not manifest anything contrary until your consciousness changes to embrace the new manifestation. The trend of your consciousness is a habit, and you change it in the same way you change any habit, by substituting a different pattern of thinking.

If you are in need of healing, the sure way to achieve it is to build a consciousness of health which is a total belief that you can be healed, a complete acceptance of health. Whether you go to a physician or to God, you must attain to a faith that you are going to be healed. Otherwise, the physician cannot heal you, nor can God. Your consciousness is an ally of prayer. It is the composite of the three phases of mind: conscious, subconscious, and superconscious; and it is the substance of your approach to all things. It determines your opinions, your concepts, your beliefs, and your manifestations.

Prayer builds a consciousness of faith. If you truly believe in the efficacy of prayer, the act of praying fortifies your belief and thus works to develop a consciousness of faith. This is all you need to insure answers to prayer, answers in like nature to that in which you ask. If you have a consciousness of faith, do not be surprised when you receive more and greater things than you ask. Your consciousness is greater than your request, and it attracts good in direct proportion to its own intensity. Miracles do not just happen. They are attracted into actuality by someone's consciousness. Just as your thoughts have power because of their relationship to the Christ within you, your consciousness is a concentration of directed power. If you would be successful in anything, first be assiduous in developing a consciousness that will believe in and accept whatever it is that you want to manifest. A consciousness not only of faith in prayer but also in the desired manifestation is a prerequisite to answered prayer.

Paul said: *Pray without ceasing.* (I Thess. 5:17) He did not mean that we must sit with eyes closed forever in meditation. He did mean that we need continuous prayerful attitudes that include a consciousness of faith in prayer and manifestation. Realize that no lack of any kind, no limitation, no stubbornly resistant demonstration can withstand the power of prayer. This is our warranty. Praying without ceasing is to maintain under all circumstances the faith that our needs are supplied, and a refusal to entertain thoughts of failure and disbelief.

In your efforts to pray without ceasing, guard against *"vain repetitions."* If you merely babble words, either aloud or silently, you are not praying. This is not communion with God. Repeating affirmations, whether long-used or original, is an excellent way to develop an affirmative consciousness, but repeat them with full realization of the Truth of the statements while meditating on their relationship to your affairs. Rattling off a list of affirmations hurriedly and without thought is fruitless.

When I was a small boy, I lived in a farmhouse in Michigan. My upstairs bedroom was unheated and very, very cold in winter. During the winter months, I began my prayer as I burst through the doorway of my room, racing toward my bed: "Now I lay me down to sleep," and I would be in bed with my head buried by the time I finished, "I pray the Lord my soul to take." I doubt that my prayers were effective. I had bounded up the stairs from the marvelously comfortable circle of heat surrounding the big coal-burning stove in the living room downstairs, and I was more concerned with getting warm again than in dallying over my prayers. Some people pray in this unthinking way all their lives, saying the words but not thinking the thoughts. Perhaps these are the people who complain that prayer does not work.

Chief Enemies

We have been trained that negatives, all negatives, are horrid. We have been taught to accentuate the positive by never entertaining a negative notion. Our training has been to a great extent salutary. The chief enemies of accomplishment are the negatives: doubt, fear, and procrastination. We ought never to dwell on negative aspects of a situation or person. Instead of failure, see success; instead of illness, see healing; instead of defects in ourselves or others, see the basic perfection. It is not in the nature of things that you can receive positive results when you present a negative consciousness.

Agreeing with all this, there is yet a place for negatives in our experience. It is the process of denial—denial of appearances. To deny the appearance of evil and to affirm the good is a powerful way to bring about the manifestation of the things or conditions we desire. Denying the power of evil sets our minds in an affirmative attitude. In this attitude our minds will then accept the truth of the positive even in the face of negatives such as limitation, illness, or other evils. However, treat denials lightly. Do not dwell on them, simply deny the appearance and call it good, and let it go. Denying a condition too strongly or too long can impress the negative condition even more deeply in our consciousness. Denial and affirmation is an accepted and effectual method of prayer that ought to be used in situations in which a negative condition looms ominously. However, after we have put out of our minds the fear of the evil by denying it, we must go quickly into a strong affirmation of good, because this is the condition we want our consciousness to accept. Always emphasize the positive.

A good indicator of self-image, as well as of faith in God, is what you ask for in prayer. If you feel "I really want this," but your consciousness tells you to be realistic and practical and you concede, "But I'll be satisfied with that," the lesser will be the high limit of your manifestation. You receive only what you can expect. The desire for achievement is part of our nature. If we believe in an ever-present and ever-loving God, then we must believe that the urge for achievement, which always prods us, continues to be directed and sustained by the Spirit of love at the core of our being. Along with an understanding of the limitless love of God for all His children comes the realization that He has decreed only the highest potential for each of us. When we settle for a lesser goal and ultimately finish with a lower station than is our desire, it is our choice, not God's. If, for example, we have a strong and continuing desire to be president of a company, we ought to accept the truth that the position is attainable. We may need to prepare ourselves, academically or otherwise, but it is yet possible. Somewhere along the line we may decide it is not worth the effort and settle for an easier job in a lower echelon. But after years of living with a gnawing sense of unfulfillment, do not blame God for the debilitating regret for "what might have been."

Specific Goals

Year by year experiences in living and working have shaped into a particular pattern your urge to achieve your potential objective. You have been led to seek your goal in business, teaching, the arts, craftsmanship, homemaking, the ministry, or any other of myriad possibilities. Whatever it is, if your highest ambition remains exciting, it is possible to you and has God's approval. Spirit has led you into experiences that have resulted in the formation of your specific goal that now occupies your mind. But if you are not satisfied with your present achievement, or promise of achievement, there is always another objective at hand that holds excitement and promise. You are never without a higher goal. And because you are a person of many talents, an objective that has proved unsatisfying can be replaced by another. Spirit has planned that you are never left empty but are always led to seek a higher accomplishment. Your ultimate goal in Spirit is the realization of your oneness with God, the oneness attained by Jesus Christ. He must ever remain before us as the ideal Man. The way to this final purpose may take devious paths and include many way stations, but we will always carry an urge toward this consummation.

You may say that not everyone can be president of a corporation, or the world's greatest painter, or physicist, or mathematician, but then not everyone wants to be any of these. But if you have a strong desire to be a leader in any field, but are discouraged by experiences and finally settle for less, remember that it is your choice, not God's. God gave you the original desire but left the rest to you. You probably attracted the disheartening experiences by your doubts and faint-heartedness. Or perhaps it was sheer laziness, or lethargy, or procrastination, or simply fright at contemplation of so high an attainment. In any event, the fact that you have not achieved your objective, or continued to desire it, cannot be ascribed as a failure of God, or that He has turned away from you. He was always with you, ready to help you achieve your goal if you would but listen and act.

There are as many individual goals as there are people, but all have one thing in common: the possibility of attainment. Every serious objective you have ever had—and you have attained many of them—has been possible to you. You came equipped with the ability, wisdom, imagination, and physical capacity to manifest any desire you can believe in. The urge you are continually receiving through your intuition is *plan big*! In order to plan big you must first think big, and this leads us back to the matter of your self-image, which is to say, your consciousness. If you impregnate your mind with the conviction that the goal you so strongly desire is yours now, just beyond the door of your mind, it is on the way to quick manifestation. This is affirmative prayer.

All of us have experienced frustration and hard work and disappointment as we move toward achievement of our ambitions. Perhaps we have come to accept the depressing belief that goals are hard to come by and inevitably require long years of labor along with deprivation and nose-to-the-grindstone dedication. Perhaps this is to some degree true, but the time of manifestation is shorter and the effort is immeasurably lighter if we work with God as our partner. We bring God into our affairs by the exercise of faith in everything we do. We are accustomed to great difficulty in achieving anything worthwhile, which may make the methods offered in this chapter seem too simple. They are not simple. The development of complete faith in your own capacities by formation of a positive consciousness is never simple or easy. It is made more difficult by disappointments of the past. Once you have attained an appropriate consciousness and self-image, the task becomes not only lighter but exciting as well.

Move Your Feet

There is excellent advice in the admonition: *Pray, and move your feet!* Sitting idly by the side of the road is not the way to get to your destination. You have an active part to play in your demonstration. This would appear elementary. You would not look to God to do everything just as you would not expect a business partner to do everything that needs to be done. Your intuition tells you the part you are to do, and if you fail to do it, your manifestation will be a long time coming. Miracles have occurred, and will occur again, "out of the blue," when seemingly one has done nothing to attract them. But an analysis will reveal that right conditions invariably were present, including a corresponding consciousness, self-image, and faith. There can be no stronger foundation for achievement of any kind, whether it is finding companionship, healing sickness, harmonizing dissension, or becoming president of a company, than faith in God who makes all things possible to those who believe. The Spirit of God is the author of your desires and the direct means of achieving them. So if you would attain your highest ambition without adulterating it by settling for a lesser and easier goal, pray to the I AM within you—your spiritual identity. Then do not fail to do whatever you are led to do to speed the manifestation.

No one can teach you to pray. It is an inside job. There is no standard formula which, once learned, insures perfect results forever, like a mathematical formula or a recipe for baking a cake. One can only remind you that the successful prayer is the prayer of faith. It is the believing prayer, and along with it you must build a consciousness—a habit of thought— that agrees with your aim. After that, you move your feet, and your hands, and your heart, and your brain. Last, and certainly not least, you act exactly as you expect to act when you attain your goal. This serves to invite your manifestation, which is even now awaiting your call.

Imagination

Imagination, the imaging power of mind, is a quality you were born with, but it is subject to development through use. Imagination may take a known set of circumstances and combine them into various forms and produce something quite different from the original. Everyone is imaginative to a degree, although some have developed the faculty to a greater proficiency than others.

You use imagination daily in the performance of every task, regardless of how ordinary or accustomed. Difficult tasks exercise your imagination more than simpler ones, and to strengthen and develop this faculty you should give it increasingly harder work to do. As your leg muscles are strengthened by walking, so is your imagination strengthened by use. Imagination is essential to prayer as well as to successful living, and it merits development.

Fanciful daydreaming requires imagination, but this kind of use is not the best training because it is not coupled with discipline. It is better to use it to aid your progress by picturing yourself in situations you can believe in, or to form images of specific accomplishment and thus build a good consciousness.

Of all the workings of the mind, perhaps the most important is imagination. Albert Einstein said: *Imagination is more important than knowledge.* There are different kinds of imagination, creative and noncreative, and not all of them are good. Some of the nonproductive forms are hallucinations, persecution complexes, hypochondria, and nightmares. Some forms of daydreaming fall into this category.

We are more concerned with creative imagination which takes ideas that are not now in evidence, perhaps never were in evidence, and builds them into usable form. Jules Verne, who scarcely strayed from his study, delighted thousands with his highly fanciful stories such as "20,000 Leagues Under the

Sea." He was criticized for writing such impossible stories, including one about a trip to the moon. Defensively he declared: *What the imagination of man can conceive, other men can achieve.* Creative imagination is far-ranging but requires training in order to soar into new patterns of thought. Samuel Morse was a portrait painter before he developed the telegraph. The first cotton gin was invented by Eli Whitney, also a painter.

Think tanks are used in industry to produce ideas. They consist of groups of men and women who gather in seclusion to develop new methods and products. Many modern advances have come out of these creative sessions. Those participating in such discussions are primarily trained in the specific industry or science in which they are called upon to work, but exhaustive training is not essential to make the creative imagination produce new and practical ideas.

Seeks New Fields

Intelligence is not a gauge of creative imagination. Some highly intelligent people may be so bound up in their own learning that their minds are not free to roam into untried channels. Imagination, by its very nature, can be controlled but not contained. It delights in flying out of its customary environment. Creativity ever seeks new fields. We know that an idea held in mind inevitably manifests itself. Manifestations are inextricably entwined with our thinking, and the quality of our manifestations is determined directly by the quality of our thoughts. Imagination is an extension of thinking, the faculty that makes it possible for us to image something of which we have no direct experience.

If we are to achieve the manifestation of a desired goal, the law of mind action requires that we hold an image of the manifestation in our minds. Since we have never previously achieved this goal, we have had no experience in what it is like. It is our faculty of imagination that builds the image by selecting other ideas and experiences, either related or unrelated, and combining them into an appropriate form. It is possible that our imagination may be incorrect and so misinform us, having been influenced by our desires and expectations. Do not be disturbed if you attain an objective and find that it is not exactly as you imagined it would be. It never is. When you reach it, your ideas will have grown and changed, and perhaps new goals will have formed in your imagination. But do not hesitate to work toward a goal because of the possibility it will not be what you now think it is. It will be close enough to satisfy you if only because it is proof of accomplishment. Any difference will be corrected by adjustments into which your imagination will lead you.

Some subscribe to the opinion that imagination is the province of the young, that only youthful persons have the resiliency to express creative imagination. This is not true. Examples abound in which both youthful and older persons have demonstrated a high degree of creativity with no definable difference in quality. The only force that can cause a diminution of creative imagination in older people is a dwindling of motivation, and this can apply as well to younger people who have given up their quest to develop new ideas or to improve their stations in life. Many great writers such as Goethe, Longfellow, and Voltaire continued to produce important works long after sixty. Milton lost his sight when he was forty-four but wrote "Paradise Lost" at fifty-seven and "Paradise Regained" at sixty-two. At seventy-one, Mark Twain wrote two books with no evidence of mental deterioration. Julia Ward Howe wrote "Battle Hymn of the Republic" at forty-three and "At Sunset" when she was ninety-one. George Bernard Shaw won the Nobel Prize when he was almost seventy. One of Thomas Jefferson's masterpieces was his appeal to Congress for the abolition of slavery, written when he was eighty-four. George Washington Carver, the southern genius who developed innumerable new products and procedures to increase agricultural productivity, was still producing new ideas with undiminished enthusiasm at eighty. Alexander Graham Bell perfected the telephone at fifty-eight, and solved the problem of stabilizing the balance of aircraft when he was past seventy.

The difference is in effort. It has been theorized that persons may lose some of their creativity in both youth and middle-age, and reduce their output of new ideas in older years because they have become bored after attaining high positions in their field and have no further urge to gain more acclaim.

Old or young, the finely honed creative imagination is the result of exercise and use. You receive ideas from Divine Mind. Goals compatible with your nature are developed within you by your creative imagination, which is the idea-gathering medium. Thinking is a divine gift; imagination is a phase of thought that makes thinking productive. As such it is limitless, and the good to be gained by its use is without limit. You can conceive of any goal you wish and your imagination will develop plans for reaching it. The more you let your imagination roam in quest of new ideas the more active, resilient, and willing it becomes. Hold in mind, believing, what you desire to have or be, and it will surely manifest.

Charles Fillmore wrote: *Everything that is manifested was first a mental picture and was brought into expression by the forming power of the imagination.* This includes not only material things such as automobiles, homes, bigger paychecks, and companionship, but also intangibles such as healing, happiness, and peace of mind. Your creative imagination works for you in everything you do, including the planning of what you desire to do. The process of goal-setting would be impossible without creative imagination, and imagination is the basic ingredient of all problem solving.

In "The Prelude," Wordsworth wrote:

Imagination is but another name for absolute power and clearest insight, attitude of mind, and Reason in her most exalted mood.

Many things in our lives cry for improvement, and the key is the application of more and better creative imagination. We are all born with this essential quality, but some develop, strengthen, and sharpen it to a greater degree than others. The infant mortality rate of ideas is enormous. Relatively few get past the first days. Thus, we watch the waste of a tremendous potential of good that will never deliver its good, either to an individual or to society, unless and until someone else attracts and accepts the same idea from Divine Mind.

Some persons deny their faculty of imagination, declaring, "I have no imagination at all. I can't even write a decent letter." It is true that one person's talents and trend of thinking differ from another's, but everyone's imagination is revealed in one way or another. Since the nature of imagination is to grow and expand and change, it is anything but static and can be developed into astonishing power, even from seeming nothingness. This is a reassuring fact when in despair we may sometimes believe that God must have passed us by when He handed out the faculty of imagination. We have an abundant supply of basic imagination, and it has the makings of an infinitely greater demonstration than it has yet shown. We can think, we can reason, we can combine ideas and experiences and develop a concept that we need. We can recall experiences of the past and use them, or variations of them, to solve present problems. What is that if it is not imagination? Some of us may feel that we lack a sufficient degree of imagination because we have allowed our minds to grow lazy and become dull and flabby. It is absolute Truth that we have dominion over our minds and can consciously direct them into any channel we choose. The mind is a marvelous instrument; it can recognize its failings and train itself into new and better ways of thinking.

He Is Creativity

We have been discussing the incredible qualities of imagination and creativity, and have outlined in simple fashion some of their accomplishing powers. These qualities are invaluable to our progress in any phase of living.

Where does creativity come from? It comes from God. He not only is creative, He is Creativity. As the Source, all the creativity in the universe must flow from Him. We are assured of our direct inheritance of all that He is, and our share of any divine faculty is governed entirely by the degree of our belief in and acceptance of it. Creativity is always available to us. We choose how much and when we will accept it.

But to say we want greater power of creativity is not enough. We must expend the effort to bring to the surface of our minds that which is now latent within them. Creativity, like the muscles of our bodies, is made supple by exercise. Train your creativity daily by making it work to develop plans, to solve problems, to originate new ideas even though the ideas do not relate to your present experience. Decide, for example, what you would do about inflation, or pollution, or how to save the endangered peregrine falcons. In such exercises, you are primarily training yourself in concentration, which no doubt is the seeming deficiency in creativity.

Meditate on the creativity of God, the creative imagination that formed all that is. Let your mind soar freely from among the forms that exist. Explore the interworkings, purposes, needs, capabilities, and potentials among the species and, as you do, realize the fullness of the Mind that created all. This is a strong exercise for your mind and imagination. As you consider the activities of people throughout the world, you will understand the limitless abundance of imagination and creativity that goes into the maintenance and progress of life each day. All people possess imagination, and all people can use it and increase its effectiveness. Most people believe that the reactions of animals are wholly instinctual, but investigation proves that some animals sometimes appear to express creativity as we define it. Instinct is a form of creativity. Who knows what will develop from it eons hence?

Like everything in your experience, your expression of creative imagination is expanded and conditioned by prayer. The prayer of faith will bring you a conviction of creativity that transposes into a powerful consciousness, enabling you to form incredible works that you never before dreamed possible.

All you need to enter into an invaluable program of self-training and prayer is motivation. This comes from a realization that creativity and imagination are essential to your life and progress, and the greater your expression of them the more prolific and satisfying are your manifestations.

A Divine Quality

The dictionary definition of imagination is: *Formation of mental images of objects not present to the senses, especially of those never perceived in their entirety; hence, mental synthesis of new ideas from elements experienced separately.* What the dictionary does not say is that imagination is a divine quality possessed by everyone as an inheritance direct from the creative Mind of God. The synthesis, or whole, frequently bears little resemblance to any of its individual parts.

To develop a new idea, you select from a reservoir of every experience, circumstance, sensation, and piece of knowledge that you have ever experienced, heard about, seen, or read, all of which are now stored in your subconsciousness. The *synthesis* your imagination produces from among these components is more than a collection of memorabilia set into form like a jigsaw puzzle; it is your expanded interpretation of them developed into new associations of form and meaning. The separate parts are seldom recognizable in the new product or idea, and this is the miraculous work of your imagination. The creativity of your nature knows what parts to select, the order in which to join them, the utilitarian interpretation of the resulting compound, and what to do with the finished product. This is called imagination.

You do not have to be a Jules Verne, an Agatha Christie, a Picasso, or an Albert Einstein to demonstrate your imagination. It moves in a vast field of inspired creativity in just plain you and me. Each time you write a note to a friend, bake muffins, fix your car, plan a vacation, or pray, your imagination takes hold with instant proficiency and dedication and does its thing. You cannot walk down the street without setting off your imagination. Imagination, the workhorse of creativity, loves to serve you, loves to be exercised.

Imagination produces a mental picture. Ideally it is a better picture than that now existing in form. This is what has brought about every improvement in the quality of life in the history of civilization. It is also responsible for every measure of progress you have made in your personal life since birth. It sets your ambitions and outlines the means of attaining them. The mental pictures limned on your consciousness by your imagination are the blueprint of your future and the promise of your tomorrows.

But in spite of its divine source and extraordinary benefits, imagination can become unruly. It can take off on an improper tangent and carry you into areas of thinking that lead to disaster. The imagination that images a successful outcome can, with equal aplomb, presage failure. It will gleefully picture the transformation of a weak and pain-wracked body into one glowing with vibrant health; or it will chronicle the psychosomatic deterioration of a healthy body into a sick one. But it is wholly under your control. If you wallow in a negative frame of mind, your imagination will romp in negation. A positive consciousness produces positive images, and your imagination would not think of fraternizing with the guttersnipes of negative thinking. As you know, images held in mind tend to manifest themselves in uncanny sameness. You know what to do with a bad image in your mind: Eject it quickly before it can do any damage.

Replace it at once with the kind of picture you want to see manifested. Although it is powerful and miracle-working, your imagination is your servant.

An Ally

Imagination is a marvelous ally in your quest for fulfillment. It follows your line of thought exactly and, by means of its dynamic creativity, develops the appropriate image and imprints it with superb clarity on your mind where it can be transposed into the outer world of form. It does even more than that: Within the boundaries set by your consciousness, it gathers supplementary ideas and includes them in the composition of the image it presents to you, strengthening and refining the picture. Under the direction of your thinking faculty, imagination makes your world, sets its boundaries, outlines its course, determines its content, and brings all into manifestation.

Imagination is a gift from God, and in the depths of your being you are eternally grateful. When you pray, give thanks for your creative imagination that images and forms the components of success and happiness in your life. Give thanks also for other gifts that make your life complete. Giving thanks is one of the purposes of prayer. It does not influence God as it might an earthly benefactor, but your expression of gratitude serves as a reminder to you of where your good comes from and directs your faith to the one Source from whom all blessings flow. "*... So, if your eye is sound, your whole body will be full of light.*" (Matt. 6:22) Pray with imagination for the widening of your horizons of good; pray for the greater use of imagination to direct your life closer to the ideal that God has in mind for you.

For An Enduring Life-Style

This is God's world, and we occupy it by the grace of Him who made it. God originated the world and everything in it, and His creativity continues to work in the myriad forms of existence. God is Spirit, and we are aware that Spirit is the ideal behind all formulated ideas, including divine potentials such as love, wisdom, power, abundance, intelligence, happiness, creativity, and all the substrata of these.

Since there is no source other than God, and we and all other forms sprang from the works of divine creativity, we must accept the Truth that all original creations are essentially good.

We were born good; our private world was good; in our minds there was no sin or evil of any kind, no hatred, no jealousy, no envy, no lack. Life was simple in expression. Although we may have had two or three instinctive fears in our genes when we were born, we were for the most part free of inhibitions.

Look what has happened to us since! We have taken an almost perfect form and twisted and warped it and piled on a host of unnatural impedimenta that have succeeded only in adulterating the beauty of the original idea, which was the newborn baby that we were. We do not remember the simplicity of life free of personality and its attendant weaknesses. To return to that pure state would mean giving up pet hates, our unbelief, and overweening pride, but it would not be giving up the sweetness of life, the joy of accomplishment, the pleasure of sensation, and the sublimity of love. These are basic and remain with us always. All good things of body and soul we would be privileged to use and enjoy. But there would be no negation, no failure, and no illness stemming from mind action, nothing to detract from our expression of freedom.

Beneath the crust of inhibitions we have accumulated, freedom exists although it seems to be well hidden. When we began to take on negation as a way of life, we went whole hog. There are countless things we fear, dislike, and neglect. Consider the good we push away, the exultation of achievement that we deny ourselves! We have built a crust of unnatural personality by allowing ourselves to be acted upon by the forces in the world.

Freedom of the Child

We would not want to live permanently as newborn babies. We like the experiences of the world, and this is good because, after all, it is God's world of accomplishment. But certainly we would like the freedom and uncalculated joy of the child. It is this that is recoverable. Life would pall without challenges, but it would be a thing of beauty if there were no insuperables. It is probably too much to expect that our lives can go back to perfection in one jump, but they can at least go far enough back to drop off inhibitions, fears, deficiencies, and other negatives. With even a few less handicaps our lives would be immeasurably improved. The removal of a handicap such as self-doubt, for example, will transform us into achieving, successful, fulfilled, and happy individuals. We were born free of all the neuroses we have developed and which now plague us. It is to this state of original freedom that we would like to return and immerse ourselves in that enduring life-style.

We have formed the habit of accepting certain things as impossible rather than following Jesus's admonition that with faith, all things are possible. We claim we cannot stop worrying, or losing our temper, or being afraid, or rid ourselves of the conviction that nothing ever works out right. This is a weakness that was surely never in the mind of the child we once were. We can return to purity and faith. With sufficient motivation we can change any habitual attitude.

All their lives people yearn for freedom as they see it, freedom to do entirely as they wish. That kind of freedom can lead to license, which is the worst bondage of all. We need not fight to acquire freedom; we were born with it. We need only to express it in ways appropriate to our environment, the only restraint being the common sense God gave us, with due thought to the good of all. When we begin to worry about what other people think of us, or whether we have the ability to cope with a situation, or whether our cold will turn into pneumonia, or whether those carefully laid plans are ridiculous, we are entering into abject slavery.

True freedom is a sublime quality that is recognizable only to spiritual insight. It is a condition of completeness in which not a shred of restraint, repression, or any other resistance exists. Of course all of us are subject to legal and moral restraints, and we must observe them if we are to claim good citizenship. But it is the subtle and very personal freedoms of our inner nature that we can take or give away as we choose. These include freedom from fear, freedom from lack, freedom from ill health, envy, hate, loneliness, and greed; freedom from all false beliefs that insinuate themselves into our minds and affairs. It is these adversaries that dominate our lives and force strong men and women to succumb to suffering.

Faith, Expectation

Some may say, "I might be able to do something about some of these things, but I can't do anything about lack of money. The way things are I can't get a better job. Also, can I help it if I catch a cold or the flu?" Let us say there is more to getting a job than walking the streets or putting an ad in the paper. Looking for employment has become a matter of strategy and finesse these days, involving a fact sheet, a prospectus, a supply of recommendations and, where appropriate, samples of work. One should always be armed with proof of ability. But the finest and most complete application may be doomed without the powerful factors of faith and expectation. Outer evidence of a good self-image is important when looking for a job. So, in many cases, something tangible can be done about lack.

It has been shown through exhaustive surveys that many of our illnesses are invited. Hypochondria is common. Lesser variations of it are countless. A consciousness of sickness will inevitably produce sickness by the forming power of thought. One is likely to "catch" whatever is going around, from influenza to shingles. The cure for this consciousness is the cure for the illness. But let us not be too hard on ourselves; none of us is perfect, and certainly we should not castigate ourselves or search our consciousness for malfunctioning if we catch a cold. On the other hand, we need to be constantly alert for the excuses our minds set up for illness and lack. Build your faith through prayer and meditation; expect health and prosperity. Help yourself by strengthening your self-image. Look always for the good, and ultimately that is all you will see. Let us keep in mind that as we think, so are we.

In "Tenure of Kings and Magistrates" Milton wrote: *None can love freedom heartily, but good men; the rest love not freedom, but license.* There are those who decry any restraint on their acts, even those imposed by law. Without law modern society would be impossible, and it is only fair that laws should apply equally to everyone. Our national constitution declares that all men are created free and equal, which is true in the matter of creation, but it has turned out that some have taken themselves into slavery through their own inhibitions and excesses, and all men have not remained equal. The pity of it is that some do not know the situation can be changed but accept the false belief that life is supposed to be burdensome and unfair and nonproductive and dull. Those are the persons who do not believe in the efficacy of prayer, or who do not listen to the voice of intuition telling them their true destiny is perfect freedom.

In previous chapters we discussed the power of our self-images, but the subject should be in every chapter and considered in relation to every aspect of our lives. In the matter of freedom, we cannot be free until we image ourselves as free. We cannot rid ourselves of any false belief until we see ourselves as being rid of it. We do it through the affirmative action of our minds. The realization that we have dominion as sons and daughters of God over our mental processes gives us the inner strength to deny slavery and to affirm freedom with respect to any trait that has enslaved us. This does not pertain only to the grave and obvious false beliefs that damage our minds, bodies, and affairs and reveal themselves to the world. It applies also to the subtle but equally grave deterrents such as envy, disbelief, fear, greed, and a multitude of small and negative reactions that join together and in the aggregate exert a tremendous force. They deny us lives of fulfillment that were ordained in us as newborn babies.

To return to the unadulterated purity of our beginning, and to preserve an enduring life-style patterned after it is the way we are given to attain the highest state our dreams can picture of life. Prayer is the way. Pray with the simple but total faith of a child that God will lead you when you place your life and affairs into His loving hands. In the life-style of purity you will be unable to hate anyone, cheat anyone, or be afraid of anyone or anything. Hold to this consciousness and you will eliminate negative habits that restrain you. New habits of faith will work miracles in attracting fulfillment of deep desires. In the quest, pray without ceasing. Some of the old habits have plagued you all your life and are stubbornly entrenched. With illumination and enough motivation, you can turn about-face when faced with a need. But afterward, the old false belief attempts to reassert itself. It will drag you back into your long-accustomed consciousness of inhibition or error. It takes much prayer and constant alertness. Pray to break the hold of the habitual thought pattern. When you pray, maintain the image in your mind of the self you want to express. Meditate on the glory and goodness of God, and invite His Spirit to permeate your consciousness until you think His thoughts and do His will in perfect assurance that you are working for your eternal good.

In this we are attempting to build a new consciousness free of the handicaps that have long held us in bondage. Handicaps such as belief in our unworthiness, doubts of our abilities, expectation of failure, and disbelief in prayer are effective blocks in our paths.

As we grow in life experiences we form trends of thought that fasten themselves to us and cling just as stubbornly as barnacles on the hull of a ship. If these attitudes of thinking are positive and lead us toward ultimate demonstrations of desired ends, we are grateful. But when our thinking dwells on limitation, we have an obligation to ourselves and to life to gain freedom by working quickly to change our consciousness.

If we are lonely and yearn for companionship, let us begin by examining our consciousness. Do we appear cold and unresponsive in our contacts with others? Are we excessively withdrawn? Are we morose and quick to anger? No one is drawn to a gloomy or irritable person. Do we believe we are not young enough, educated enough, handsome enough, rich enough, bright enough to encourage acquaintances to become friends? Do we really like people?

These are barnacles that need to be scraped

off our minds. The son of God is not subject to these implications, and if any are apparent they are lies against our true nature. Know who you are. If you consider yourself unsuccessful in any phase of living, know that this is entirely foreign to the nature of God and therefore has no place in you. Looking at these unpleasant false beliefs is not to smear our self-image but to stir in us the determination to assert our divine right to happiness.

Expect It, Get It

No doubt you know people who expect a cold every spring and every fall, and frequently between; sure enough, they catch a cold every spring and every fall and frequently between. They expect it to last two weeks, and it lasts two weeks. It is never fatal because they do not expect it to be fatal, but it is fully as uncomfortable as they anticipate. This may appear a little farfetched, but actually it is not. Our intuition instructs us that it is not the will of God that we be sick. If you seem to be subject to periodic colds, you can guard against them by praying defensively. You can prevent a cold more easily than you can cure one, by prayer. Start by thanking

God for perfect health. See yourself expressing vibrant well-being and youthful vitality,
enjoying a clear head. Hold this thought and
no doubt you will beat the next cold. And you
will not have to stay out of the rain and keep
your feet dry.

When my wife and I took the canoe trip
down the Yukon River a few years ago, our
feet were wet the entire three months. We
had no thought of catching colds, and we did
not. On that trip we met an Athapascan In-
dian who lived a solitary life beside the river
forty miles from his nearest neighbor, sub-
sisting off the land and river. I asked him
what he would do alone in the wilderness if he
became ill. "I don't get sick," he retorted.
"Who am I to catch sickness from, a moose?"
With that consciousness he will live a long
life.

I spent several years as a traveling salesman, selling fountain pens and mechanical
pencils. One of my customers was a small-
town druggist. This customer was surrounded daily by remedies of every descrip-
tion, and he needed most of them for his own
ailments. He verged on hypochondria. I ac-
cused him of getting sick so he could take
some new pill to see if it would work. On one

of my calls he had just been released from a hospital. After exhaustive tests the doctor had told him he was very allergic to medication he had taken for arthritis. He was thoroughly scared and told me he was not going to take any more pills. Strangely enough his arthritis had almost disappeared when I last saw him. He held to his program and henceforth had fewer illnesses.

There is a pristine beauty in our nature that is unsullied by experience, by years, even by negative thinking. It is with us when we are born and when we decide to die. It is the eternal Spirit of God which never gets tired, never grows old, never wears out. Our bodies wear out and grow old because we cannot be convinced that this Spirit is our spirit, the essence of our Self and the sustainer of our life. Spirit is as strong within us when we are ninety-nine as when we are nineteen; it is the eternal divinity at the core of our being. We grow old not only because we think it is the thing to do but also because we want to grow old. Scientists have never found the bug that would explain the reason that our marvelous, incredible, self-perpetuating bodies should ever deteriorate. But scientists have never dissected the negative consciousness and found the power there. That's the bug.

Age seems to sneak up on us. One day we find a gray hair, and that day we realize that we are getting along in years. Gone are the days of our youth and vigor and good times. We yank out the offending hair and watch fearfully but expectantly for the next one. That is the day we begin to slow down, to tire more easily, and to feel our years. Yesterday we were young; today we are old. We insist that yesterday we were deluding ourselves and today we are being realistic. After all, we are getting gray, and we are not kids any longer. Suddenly it seems all our friends are talking about their aches and reminiscing about how it used to be when they were young. Some live longer than others, much longer, but no one yet has completely escaped the grinding down of time. Perhaps we just get tired of living.

What a Life!

Now is this any way to live? Is this any way to return the favor of life to God who is eternal and who placed His eternal Spirit within each of us? Does anyone think of praying for the return of fresh, vigorous, and dynamic youth?

Prayer taps the No. 1 power in the universe. That power works equally in every situation, large and small. The prayer of faith never fails. Yet people will tell you that prayer does not work. They know because they have tried it, and even when it works they will not believe. If you remind them that their prayer was answered they will tell you, "Oh, I did that myself. I tried one more time, and it came through." Or, "Things just worked themselves out. It would have happened anyway." Though they may have tried for years to bring about the answer, they refuse to concede that it could have come from an esoteric, intangible thing like Spirit. They saw no bolts of lightning, heard no crashing thunder; the ground did not shake with earthquakes; they experienced no seizures or faintings; no ghosts appeared. The thing they had been seeking just happened. Just like that. Some people are actually too proud to admit that anything beyond their own efforts can produce beautiful results. Such people need to be reminded it is their own effort that does it—a great desire plus a spark of faith.

Let us remember that answers to prayer do not always come as miracles. The disciples had been out on the water all night and had come in with empty nets. Jesus told them to go out once more. They climbed into their boat, no doubt with faith and expectation, and when they returned their nets were overflowing. Without faith, there is no prayer. The faith-filled prayer is always answered, if not today then tomorrow when we have more faith. When you pray, do not pray to prove that prayer works. This would mean that you fear that prayer may not work, or probably will not work, and if it does, the results will not be distinct enough to serve as proof. If you are praying to God, He does not need proof that prayer works; if you are not praying to Him, to whom are you praying? Negatives add up to negatives, and negatives have no part in successful prayer. Do not pray in desperation, but in confidence. Desperation means that you are afraid that your prayer will not be answered, or answered in time. That is not the way to approach your Father, He who is even now waiting with outstretched hands with gifts for your acceptance.

Meditate before you pray. Still the turmoil in your heart. Let fear drain away and faith surge in. In a consciousness of faith let your wants be known to God, realizing at the same time that He already knows, but now you are ready. Then stand back and watch the demonstration happen. Deep prayer brings a sense of peace and fulfillment that you can scarcely find in the same intensity any other way. Prayer makes you feel good, and if there were no other answer than that, your prayer would be worthwhile. When you "feel good" your mind expands, love comes into your heart, and you are satisfied with yourself and your world. How often do we attain such a state of contentment when our problems seem nonexistent or easily solvable and all things are bright and beautiful? When you feel good your mind is right, which makes your affairs right, and this is the whole formula. Prayer, then, has double value: it makes you feel good and at the same time produces the answer you want. Pray for the good feeling, and hold the thought. This is the way to a good life.

We have come a long way since the first day of our lives. The way has been dappled with joys and disappointments, perhaps more of one than the other, and the proportion is governed by how often we feel good about ourselves. All of us need to return to the unblemished simplicity of our beginning, to remind ourselves of the basic pristine beauty out of which we have grown. We were born new beings, yet old. New in potential, old in soul. We have been searching for our potential in the context of our souls ever since, and we have been directed by the voice of Spirit all our lives. Perhaps we have not always listened or, having listened, obeyed. When we agreed with our intuition, our paths became smooth and our way successful. It is this life-style of at-one-ment that is the goal of every son and daughter of God.

We stumble and fall because of our own small view of ourselves. Self-flagellation gives one an inferiority complex. No one is inferior, but some appear to believe they are. It is the curse of frustration that it too often fastens the burden of false beliefs on our minds. Of all the components of a bad self-image, perhaps the most devastating is the sense of inferiority. We were not born with it, but along the way we have foolishly allowed ourselves to become mired. We would be in a sad state, hopelessly outclassed in our competition for survival, if we actually were inferior; but if we believe it, the effect is the same. There is perhaps no greater handicap to successful living than a sense of inferiority. It is our personal enemy. It causes us to downgrade our talents and attainments, not only to others but to ourselves, which robs us of confidence. If you have a feeling of inferiority, you must gain a new perspective of yourself; and this is easier than you might believe. It takes more, however, than superficial treatment. This rock-hard attitude can be broken by a reversal of mind.

What is your concept of God? Do you look upon Him as one who can be influenced for you or against you? Do you believe His almightiness is subject to error and that He made a mistake in your case? Do you believe that you lack some of the saving qualities of God that others possess? Do you believe that after you were created God forgot you and left you to fend for yourself? Do you actually believe that you are alone in the wilderness of an unfriendly world without God's guidance and support? These questions sound ridiculous. And they are. Yet the person in bondage to an inferior complex appears to answer yes to all of them. But you know intuitively that God is impersonal Spirit and sows His blessings equally upon all His creation. He is love, power, wisdom, intelligence, and joy, and He has always been present within us with all His qualities. Likewise, He is present in all other persons. You were not shortchanged in natural attributes when you were born. So what happened?

Perhaps you will say, with partial illumination, "Of course I believe all this, but it is what I have done with my life that makes me inferior." Now we are getting down to fundamentals. Do you believe, for example, that you do not have enough education to compete with other people? Opportunities for advanced education are open to you. So there goes that crutch. You have agreed that you have been given your share of intelligence with the presence of the Spirit of intelligence abiding within you. It may be possible that through environmental or other factors you have not developed it. Your seeming handicaps may lead us to understand your problem but not wholly to excuse it. You need not look far to find other persons with infinitely greater handicaps who have outgrown them. Do not shoot arrows at God or at society. God gives you Himself, all of Him that you will ever need, and society is, like the farmer's field, available to you to till and reap the harvest. You have a responsibility to yourself and to your Creator to make use of the gifts you received in the beginning to attain the potential revealed in the goals and desires you were given at the same time.

No Blame!

This is part of the problem of inferiority. Such people are loaded with the uncomfortable feeling that with a little more effort they could have made more out of their lives, reached higher goals. Couldn't we all! But not all of us do waste time sitting by the wayside blaming everyone, including ourselves. Life is a vast wasteland of unfulfilled dreams for those who have resigned themselves to second-rate expression of their capacities, and who have chosen to wallow in mediocrity and belief in inferiority. Such persons will make no effort, either because of habit, hopelessness, or lethargy. They will be inferior in self-expression though equal to others in the qualities that make up their Self. It is those who rebel at a sense of inferiority who prove the love and power of God. They are those who go back to school, who nurture and train their faith, who make the effort, who force aside their timidity and plunge into participation, even leadership, who make themselves proceed with projects that they have felt were beyond them, who take advantage of their own worth and give themselves the chance to realize their dreams. They will discover they are equal, if different, from those they have heretofore envied.

But after the blinders have fallen from our eyes and we have caught a glimpse of the potential blessings that have suddenly become available, we must take immediate steps to stabilize the dream. It must be safeguarded and perpetuated, else it may be transitory like a puff of smoke drifting past and soon gone. Prayer and understanding will hold the gain. Prayer is a needed component of any effort to establish oneself as an equal member of God's world. Without the inner assurance that the attempt is possible of success, that our faith is well-founded, we will not be able to give the effort the required enthusiasm.

Meditate on God. See Him clearly as the Supreme Being, the God of love, who has bestowed His blessing upon you in large measure. He is your Father and has set His Spirit within you. Your prayers are heard, welcomed, and answered. Know that you are an essential entity in the world, created to play a part in the forward and upward movement of mankind with ultimate fulfillment of the divine purpose.

It may seem an infinitesimal role that an individual plays, but any personal achievement or expression in the pattern of one's own nature adds to the total of the world's progress. Everyone has a work to do, and you have yours, which makes you an essential part of the community of man. This is in the ideal. Failure to progress toward your personal goals is denying the world the harvest you have to offer. This does not pertain only to business, or to works of art, or producing an invention that would add to the comfort or convenience of the world's people. It applies also to simple achievements like becoming a good craftsman or artisan or farmer or housewife, or attaining the eminence of being a truly good person. If you fulfill your own nature, you fulfill the will of God.

When the realization of your intimate relationship with the omnipresent Creator sweeps over you, you no longer can hold deprecating thoughts about your own worth. And when you go on to consider the achievements you have made in the development of

God's plan for you, you will be proud and grateful and self-fulfilled.

Now you have improved your self-image. See yourself as an important member of society with a great potential, riding the wings of Spirit toward the attainment of your deep desires which also are the desires of God. You suddenly find yourself free of the shackles of inferiority. You take your place with confidence.

Periodically, we all ought to read the parable of the Prodigal Son in Luke 15:11-32. In it we find the history of our own experiences. It is a lesson to be learned. In a manner of speaking, all of us are prodigal sons; we had our beginnings in our Father's house; but, lured by sensation, we turned away from it and journeyed to a far country. Even if we did not waste our substance in riotous living, we yet adulterated our consciousness with errors and inhibitions that diverted our path, straying far from the sweetness and purity that characterized the children we once were. Now, like the Prodigal Son in the parable, we are on our way home. Our Father is waiting with the fatted calf and the ring and the robe to celebrate our return. His gifts to us include peace, abundance, fulfillment, and joy. Perhaps we are among those who are not conscious of returning to the Father but are working our way back through expression of His divine attributes in our way of life. Our Father asks only that we do not remain strangers to Him and His will, that we do not waste His precious gifts in unproductive endeavors. God does not punish us for willfulness or for mistakes; our failure to manifest the bountiful blessings God has for us is punishment enough. If we misuse or fail to use our talents, it is we who suffer the resultant limitation.

Returning to the Father's house and receiving His bounty bears certain responsibilities; we must obey the rules of the house if we are to continue to abide there. First, we are to recognize love as the abiding principle of life—love of God, love of ourselves as spiritual beings, love of our neighbor, love of all good. Love for ourselves does not mean conceit or narcissistic love, but rather a good feeling about ourselves without a sense of inferiority or condemnation. Love for God does not mean to love Him for what we can get from Him but to love Him for what He is, which is quite a different thing. It means to love the good for good's sake. It means to appreciate Him as wisdom, power, joy, peace, health, and abundance. Love these qualities in their divine nature and you love God. The rules of the house are stringent but not oppressive. Return to the Father's house and become a good member of the family and you will forevermore live the good life of contentment in the beatific state in which every good desire is fulfilled. This possibly sounds incredible now, but it will become less so as you meditate on the nature of God and on the transforming power of His love.

This is what I mean by an enduring lifestyle of good. It is a return to God, a return to our original state of the ideal, in which we were close to the heart of Him who created us, and expressing the unadulterated purity of the Christ. Do not let the awesome height of perfection frighten or dishearten you. Since Jesus Christ, no one has achieved it wholly, but countless people are on the path upward, shedding their failings one by one. In proportion to the closeness of their approach to God, they enter into a beautiful expression of life. We do not have to be perfect; but if we want to notably improve our situation, we had better be on our way!

Authority

Moses, a wise and great man, wrote in the first chapter of Genesis, verse twenty-six: *Then God said, "Let us make man in our image, after our likeness; and let them have dominion . . . ."*

And God did this thing; He created us in His image and after His likeness, and He gave us dominion over all things of the Earth, and the sky, and the sea. And He instilled His Spirit within our very beings so that we have dominion over our minds, which is to say, over ourselves and our world. Dominion over our minds means total control of mental processes, of the interpretations it makes of various and conflicting experiences. These interpretations have since strayed from the truth as we have become influenced by our humanness. Our interpretations have fed on their own waywardness and developed faulty, even perverse, concepts that have diverted us from our divine destinations. Yet we were given eternal dominion over them—today, tomorrow, and forever.

The text *"in our image, after our likeness"* means that we are like God in all ways, from the very depths of our being to the utmost perimeters of consciousness. It does not mean that we are God. It means that we are like God, partaking of His nature and His qualities and His Truth. He bestowed upon us His authority so that we may have dominion over our world.

Personal Will

If He gave us individuality in Him, which must include unassailable dominion over our minds and bodies and over the affairs of our world, what has happened to our authority? We say that in Truth nothing is impossible to God, but one thing He cannot do, or chooses not to do, is to usurp our personal will.

The responsibility for our well-being is ours. We were supplied all needed equipment, including authority, to make our lives beautiful and joyous, with full expression of Self. What we do with it is our decision. God's will for us is good, all good, nothing but good. He wants for us what we want for ourselves. With all this going for us, it would seem that our way is easy and our burden is light. It is easy in the ideal, but frequently it is quite different in the actual. However, the solution to any problem we may have is clear. It is to return to God and abide in His law and obey His counsel. Independence is generally a good quality; it is the foundation of personal progress and the motivation for any new venture. But when it leads us away from the counsel of the Christ Mind and into ways foreign to our higher nature, it becomes willfulness or stubbornness, which are adversaries of good.

You can trust Divine Mind to know what is good for you, and you can trust your divinely inspired intellect to carry out successfully the will of God for a life of joy, health, and plenty.

A question common to many, in regard to seeking Spirit guidance, is: How can I be sure of knowing what God's will is? It seems that we ought to know. With the understanding that Spirit is integrated throughout our being, even to the far corners of our consciousness, we may wonder why we are not aware of the will of God. The truth is that we do know and always have known. We know through our intuition, which is the voice of God speaking to us in the form of hunches. Intuition is our guide and contact with Spirit, from whom we receive divine counsel. We can, and sometimes do, misinterpret the instructions of our intuition through the influence of our ungoverned will, and thus we are led into paths of limitation. But there is help even for this, although our wayward nature and stubborn concepts and deluded minds may offer resistance. Our help comes in prayer.

The Answer

In prayer we find the answer to all problems. In prayer we speak to God, the source of wisdom. Not only do we speak to Him but, ideally, we listen more than we speak. He already knows our wants and seeks entry into our minds to provide guidance. Open-minded prayer, free of tension, stubbornness, and preconceived answers, will reveal the right course.

It is quite possible to pray and then to misinterpret the answer. Let us remind ourselves that we are to evaluate the answers to prayer. Let us be sure that we have heard the voice of God and not the voice of our stubborn will. And let us continue to pray and keep our minds open and let the will of God become strong in consciousness. Once-in-a-while prayer or one-day-a-week prayer are not enough. We need to pray without ceasing by ever listening for guidance from within, more than from without. We do not want to fight our intuition, for it is the guiding, protecting, loving voice of Spirit. But we will pray until guidance becomes conviction; then we will know we have interpreted rightly.

Listen to the true voice, and with faith. When you get a hunch from the depths of your being, you are prodded to obey it. It is right for you, and you must obey. Prove it by letting it grow and establish itself in your consciousness. Deny it at the peril of your progress. Do not allow a pet belief or timidity to rob you of your inheritance. Follow your intuition, work at it, and thank God for His compassion and loving care.

Working hand in hand with intuition is the way to express our God-given authority. We carry out instructions from within through our spiritual power of imagination, which shapes situations to our needs. In the beginning we were given authority to control all that concerns us, to manifest the full potential of success and happiness, and to protect ourselves from negative factors in the world. Remember, however, our authority is only over our own consciousness. The work is done in faith and the imaging power of mind. Image only the good you want to see manifested, and only that will remain.

Read again the first chapter of Genesis, verse twenty-six: ... *"Let us make man in our image, after our likeness; and let them have dominion...."* In the image and after the likeness of God we were formed, and we have dominion. Not realizing this, some of us frequently abdicate our position of authority and allow ourselves to be driven by the fitful breezes of chance or fallacy, which inevitably carries us into limitation or defeat. But let us never forget that we have inherent dominion. Through the exercise of natural authority over our thinking processes, we can lift ourselves out of any repressive situation. Our authority is without limit because it is designed by the Most High. It accompanies us into the world and is expressed in the positive action of our minds. We think and believe, and that which we believe is manifested. This is total dominion.

Belief, Authority

Act with authority. Believe that you have authority over ill health and limitation and debilitating habits of thought. Your authority will work swiftly to destroy them. Doing this will convince your doubting nature that truly you are in control.

How many times have you said, "I wish I could be different; I wish I could get rid of that habit; I wish I had the strength to stave off the problems that keep coming into my life; I wish I could be healthy and prosperous and loving; I wish I could overcome"? These things are easy. But if you don't know your power, or knowing it don't assert it, you are as helpless as though divine authority had never been incorporated into your being.

Our minds are long entrenched in the habit of taking orders from all manner of bosses. Ill health, lack, frustration, inharmony, envy, and a host of other unpleasant emotions line up to give us a whack as we run the gauntlet in our daily living. All the while they have no real power over us. Through our supine unassertiveness we actually beg them to take control and knock us about at will. Thus, we indict ourselves and pronounce a life sentence of repression and slavery. When understanding flows into our minds as a clear stream, unsullied by habitual mesmerism, we are struck with the jolting realization that we have given away our birthright. A phantom monster, foreign to our nature, has taken over. Self-delusion fades before understanding. Understanding is an intuitive assurance that comes from meditation on our relationship with God.

God makes no mistakes. He created you perfect. In His sight you are whole and complete in divine attributes. Never underrate your noble birth. You came into the world with a royal inheritance of dominion. Your regal authority is undeniable, although revolutionary conditions promulgated by your own negative reactions are working to undermine your position of power. But your innate authority, though latent, is invincible. It does not wear out from use, nor does it rust from nonuse. It is as strong now as it has ever been and as it ever shall be. Let your authority be justified by recognition and utilization.

Your demonstrations leading to success

and happiness rise from your consciousness, and your consciousness is formed from your habitual thought. This is so obvious that it is trite to say it again, but it bears repeating because of its importance. If your life conditions are not now to your liking, it is because your habitual thinking is on the wrong track. You can set it right by taking authority over your mind. This is a great and important authority because your mind makes your world. The ideas that control your mind also control you.

An Unpopular Fellow

I had a friend who was basically an agreeable fellow, but as a protection against others he perceived as taking advantage of him, he assumed a dictatorial facade. He held this attitude so long that it became a full-time habit, not a particularly comfortable one, but a habit he lived with because it seemed to cover his vulnerability. My friend was unpopular and disliked by many of his fellow workers. Because he was a brilliant man, his employers promoted him several times for their own advantage. Promotions brought a certain pride and more pay but no real satisfaction. He attained a high place but occupied a lonely eminence. Shunned by others, even by his superiors, he became embittered. His long-continued autocratic attitude altered his personality, and he no longer consciously remembered that originally it had been a device to protect him from certain strong individuals with whom he believed he was in competition.

When he was named to a top management position, he felt that he had attained his goal. Nevertheless, he was vaguely dissatisfied. There were few congratulations and no celebration at the office. He could not even celebrate privately in his home. His attitude reached into his private life and brought strained relations with his family. Although he had acquired certain authority over others, he could not claim dominion over his own mind. He did not realize what was wrong and did not know how to correct the situation, which he did not understand. He felt that somehow he was a misfit.

But as many of us, he came to believe that everyone else was at fault. Even though he did not fit into the social structure, he felt that people shouldn't shun him. He told himself that certainly he was knowledgeable in his job, and efficient, and fair to those serving under him. Although my friend had attained a position of success, and it could be said that he had demonstrated dominion over his affairs, in a larger sense he was totally in bondage to his emotions. He had forgotten how to get along with people.

He took early retirement. Regardless of his important contribution to the company's success, his going-away party was sparsely attended, and a diamond watch was presented to him with faint eulogy.

Release Comes

Now that he was released from pressure, released from competition, he gradually found release in his mind. It seems such a simple thing to change one's attitude in personal relationships, just a matter of dropping a stiffly autocratic approach and substituting one of friendly understanding. But after years of living with a staunch habit, it meant tearing out by the roots old, established concepts that clung stubbornly in his mental processes.

Retirement brought automatic relaxing. In fact, he congratulated his successor and even offered to go to the office and help him get acclimated to the job. Now that he no longer had his job or prestige to protect, his personality began to change. Old habits hung on for a while because his consciousness did not suddenly change. He made no conscious effort to reform; the change came about when the hard knots of suspicion and fear dropped from his mind. Months later he finally came to the realization that his attitude had been the culprit. He always had believed in hunches, and now he had a strong leading to improve his relations with others. He went about it with enthusiasm. His attempts were awkward at the beginning, but his true nature began to emerge, to the astonishment of his acquaintances. "Old Ben has turned out to be a really nice guy," one said. He became active in service organizations and found that he enjoyed it. A year later he served without pay as counsel for his former employer's research department. It is a pity, his co-workers said, that Ben couldn't have acted like this years ago.

All his life Ben had fought a poor self-image. No one knew the agonies he had suffered in his climb to success.

When the blocks were removed, the Spirit

of God moved in with guidance and love. Ben did not know that the Christ Spirit within him was responsible for his change of heart; but Spirit demands no credit. When we open our minds and hearts for guidance, God's wisdom flows in, and we are blessed. Perhaps those of us who have discovered the source of our good are more fortunate than Ben because we are ready now to move into lives of fulfilled potential. Let us be grateful for this illumination which makes the presence of God a mighty guide and protector.

When one has a problem, the best advice anyone can give is this: Deliberately take control of the situation rather than allowing it to control your mind. You need not try to take control alone. Call upon God. Ask for His sure guidance so your personal consciousness will not lead you into wrong action. God will respond with strength and wisdom. Your partnership with Him can do no wrong. Let your partnership embrace every facet of your life, all that you need to give you serenity and a sense of accomplishment.

The Christ, our I AM identity, is our power and authority. Christ is the activity of God within us. Treasure the authority of the Christ, which is of God and from God. Paul wrote to the Colossians: . . . *Christ in you, the hope of glory.* (Col. 1:27) Christ is our assurance of completeness, demonstrating the fullness of the heritage that is ours by virtue of our birth. Paul also wrote, in Philippians 4:13: *I can do all things in him who strengthens me.* You and I also can do all the things we need to do through Him who strengthens us and makes our efforts productive. Jesus Christ is our Way-Shower, the model of man expressing his divinity, the proof of the miraculous dominion God gave His highest creations.

Proof of Authority

With all this proof of authority, how can we fail to believe it? It is clear and unequivocal. We have proved it innumerable times in our experience, yet we refuse to accept the position of authority in the most important areas of our lives—the manifestation of our highest dreams and the denial of limitation. We appear to be awed by our own hopes. "Too good to be true" is a common feeling we have for the most significant among our dreamed-of objectives. How blind can we be? The promises of Jesus Christ, which are the promises of God, ought to be our perfect assurance that all we can ask of Spirit and of life is ours. It is ours before we ask, having been born with us in an unformed state ready to manifest on demand. Our prayer is our demand. The prayer of faith, along with expectation and active acceptance demonstrated in preparation for receiving, is the magic formula for bringing forth into fact every good desire of our hearts.

Prayer is the way, the unfailing way. If we have prayed and have been denied, the only possible reason is that we have prayed amiss. Perhaps we have prayed without believing, without expectation, without enthusiasm and joy, without taking an active part in the demonstration.

There are many components of faith in prayer. First, there is the belief that what we ask is possible to us. Second, we must have no doubts that we are worthy. Third, faith demands that we possess the ability to receive and to cope with the manifestation. We must not fear or waver or grow impatient. Above all, we must believe. James addressed the twelve tribes, saying: *But let him ask in faith, with no doubting, for he who doubts is like a wave of the sea that is driven and*

*tossed by the wind. For that person must not
suppose that a double-minded man, unstable
in all his ways, will receive anything from the
Lord.* (James 1:6-8) In prayer a double-
minded man is one who sees both manifestation and failure, and this weakens his prayer.
While praying for an answer, he accepts the
possibility that there will be none, and if the
favorable answer does not appear quickly,
the little faith he has fades, and he feels the
probability that there will be no response.
That is no prayer at all. Be strong in your
faith. Ask boldly, and do not be afraid to ask
big. Without a breath of doubt, expect God to
answer your prayer and pour out more and
better than you ask for. That is the largesse
of Spirit.

Our dominion over the world is a yeasty
passion that demands release into activity. It
seeks its own consummation through us. It is
not a passive thing that lies quiescent until
we call for it; but, like a divine idea, it is insistent and demands expression. Unsatisfied desires never give us rest. We are not satisfied
if we have failed to demonstrate authority in
any confrontation with our desires.

Many older persons are haunted by "what
might have been." Let us not prepare to look

back later in regret that we did not exercise our authority to subdue recalcitrant circumstances in the past. Our deeply held desires will gnaw at us long after we have given up expecting them to come to pass. Act now! To delay is to prolong the dissatisfaction, to hold at a distance the demonstration you long for, to suppress longer your spirit that cannot accept suppression but must surge against its prison bars to your eternal discomfort.

We bring authority and dominion to bear through prayer, always through prayer. Develop the proper perspective toward prayer by understanding its qualities and purposes and powers. Charge your mind with faith and joy and expectation and gratitude. Do this and you will pray aright, and there will follow the inevitable demonstration of spiritual dominion over the large and small concerns of your life.

Thank God for His gift of His authority. Without dominion we would be subject to the vagaries and whims of every person, circumstance, event, and condition of the world, and we surely could not prevail. If we do not recognize and use our divine authority, we will find negative forces aligned against us, and we will suffer frustration. Dominion over mind and its reactions, however, renders persons and circumstances benign; they cannot harm or repress us. Instead, in them we find our ultimate attainment. God's power is our power coming forth from Him, not to bend persons or even outer conditions to our will but to attract the good that is in them. All people are one in Spirit, and unless they take themselves out of the mainstream, they interchange blessings for the benefit of each and all.

Remind yourself that the only authority you possess is over your own mind. That is the only authority you ever will need, for the conditions under which you live reflect your thoughts. You are precisely what you think, no more and no less. It is a cumulative effect; you are not necessarily what you think at this moment but what you have thought habitually. The wheels grind slowly as your mind changes slowly. If you have lived for a considerable time with certain inhibitions, you have formed habits of response which in turn have molded the affairs of your life. If you wish to change the molds, you can do so as quickly as you can substitute a new habit of thinking. No one ever said it is easy, but it is a work of joy. It is a joy to watch the conditions of your life improve, your long-awaited answers appear, your frustrations fade. It takes understanding and motivation. It takes prayer to convince yourself to open the gate of your mind to God. This also requires the other factors we have been discussing—a good self-image, faith in yourself and in your goal, faith in your worthiness and your ability. Don't shrink from the job because the effort seems too great. When you emerge from the far end of the tunnel, you will look back and think how easy it all was! You will have transformed your mind.

Good Is Now

God's work is instantaneous. It is we who take so long. Our good is now waiting for us to get around to calling it forth.

Gain the realization that God wants all of us to prosper and be wholly happy. If it were not true, He would not have given us the ability and the dominion, both of which we possess as natal gifts.

We are made in God's image of perfection. What have we done with that image? We must return to it through dedication to prayer. Along with His image comes authority to manifest the blessings of Spirit in accordance with God's nature. This is our destiny and our ultimate goal. It is our obligation to the Creator and to His creation. It is not an oppressive obligation. Through it we claim the greatest joy and exultation possible. This is our gift, and it is ours to possess and use through the grace of God. In no more beautiful way does God's love come to His children.

Prayer Therapy

In your study of Truth you have come to see the reality of many things that once seemed far removed from your experience. Some of these are that prayer can heal a sick body, a sick mind, and any problem. Those who deny the power of prayer to do today what Jesus Christ demonstrated 2,000 years ago deny the power of God. Jesus proclaimed to the multitude: *"Truly, I say to you, many prophets and righteous men longed to see what you see, and did not see it, and to hear what you hear, and did not hear it."* (Matt. 13:17) The power of prayer is a vast energy hidden from men and women only when they refuse to see.

Jesus healed people with all kinds of problems. He restored life to the lifeless. And He said: *"... he who believes in me will also do the works that I do; and greater works than these will he do, because I go to the Father."* (John 14:12)

The potential to heal is ours to demonstrate. How do we attain this marvelous authority over our ills? By prayer, of course. It cannot be a weak-kneed prayer, a doubting prayer, a fearful prayer. It should be a strong, confident, never-doubting, affirmative prayer. We need to pray the way Jesus prayed, in His nature and power.

Where to Begin

We begin by clearing our minds of doubt. Then we *feel* the healing taking place. We see perfection where there seemed to be imperfection, and we speak words of healing. Never again do we see the appearance of the problem as true, but as a perversion of the truth, subject to the power of our word. Do not supplicate God; this indicates fear that He will not heal you. *Thou shalt also decree a thing, and it shall be established unto thee....* (Job 22:28 A.V.) This is not begging. Decree not with belligerence, but with conviction. When you decree a thing, you *know* it is going to come about. Health in your mind, body, and affairs is an idea in Divine Mind and, as such, is demonstrable. Never is there a lack of health, only *an appearance of lack.* You can draw upon health, decree it forever, and never deplete the supply at the Source. Memorize this affirmation: *In the nature and through the power of Jesus Christ, I decree vitalizing energy throughout my body, and I am healed.* See the power at work, watch the healing being done, rejoice in it, and give thanks. Erase forever non-healing thoughts from your consciousness.

The traditional job of a physician is to heal illnesses, but a physician admittedly does not heal. Our bodies heal themselves through self-restoring, self-perpetuating faculties that are innate in every cell. The physician is necessary for arranging circumstances so that the body may proceed with its healing. Perhaps a physician's most noteworthy service is to listen to us and assure us that all is not lost.

Only God heals. He heals through His gift of self-renewal. His healing is done through the inspired minds of men and women who accept His powerful therapy. A great many scientists and others, including Charles Fillmore, have concluded that illnesses have their source in error concepts in our minds. Permanent healing cannot be accomplished until the cause of sickness—error consciousness—is erased. Ailments are cured by ferreting out offending concepts or attitudes and bringing them into the bright light of spiritual understanding. So long as we hold to error consciousness we prolong illness.

A Tough Lesson

A number of years ago, I was heavily involved in my business, working, as the saying goes, night and day. Because of the never-ending deadlines of the business, there was never time for a vacation. Finally, my wife and I used a day before and after a holiday and drove from our central California home to Los Angeles to visit our daughter. I felt harried, tense, and guilty that I had deserted my office for even this brief time. As we drove, I said to my wife, with great feeling, "I need a rest! I wish we could get away for a while with nothing to do but sit!" I was serious about it, although my consciousness was such that I could see no prospect of taking extended time off.

Within an hour, we were involved in an

accident in which I sustained a broken back. My wife was tossed about, but her injuries were less serious than mine. So I got my rest, four months of it, one month in the hospital and three at home.

Some would say it was simply a coincidence; I just happened to express my desire for rest and get hurt the same evening. If so, it was a strange coincidence. I believe I attracted what I decreed and, as frequently happens, I got more than I asked. Perhaps you might ask if God would do such a thing to you, one of His children? Break your back? Put you in the hospital for a month? Couldn't He have arranged a vacation in a less dramatic and painful way? I did not say that God broke my back. He did not. And I did not ask Him to give me a vacation. I simply stated, under great stress, that I had to get away for a rest, and impersonal Principle acted swiftly to provide me a long one.

This experience taught me two lessons— never drive without my seat belt being fastened, and never deliberately decree something I don't want to manifest.

I am glad to report that I was healed permanently. In fact, my doctor told me that the break-point is now the strongest part of my back. My wife also has had no aftereffects.

I do not pretend to know how Principle works, although I think I know why it works. It worked in this case because I desired it so vehemently, and the answer arrived quickly in response to my decree. It is the same as when one talks of hard times and unemployment. Fearing them, one can sometimes wind up poor and jobless. When one says, "I'm allergic to grass," one almost always gets the sniffles when near it. Assuredly, God does not fire us from our jobs and take away our money, nor does He send pollen to make our heads stuffy, nor does He in a pique withhold His answer to our prayers until we learn to have more faith. But what we believe and decree, we receive. It works the opposite way, too. The prayer of faith brings the results we want, typically multiplied. An expression of goodwill for another, spoken or felt, brings an abundance of the same in return. A firm belief in the healing power of God can lift from our bodies feelings of lethargy and make us strong and vital, and if we backslide momentarily and contract an ailment, our habitual faith makes the illness brief.

Miracles of healing are occurring all about us, some unheralded and without public notice. They happen because people pray. People heal themselves and others by prayer. After observing healings accomplished miraculously and against great odds, we are led to say with Jesus Christ: ... *"All things are possible to him who believes."* (Mark 9:23)

Who Is Responsible?

In instances of healing, whose beliefs effect the change, the person who is ill or the person who prays? The person who is ill surely believes. One who prays for another's healing speaks from the love and power of the Christ Mind within him, directing his prayer to the Christ in the other, and the Christ performs the healing. There is agreement between the pray-er and the prayed-for. The sick person acquiesces, and the healing power works unencumbered by fear and disbelief. He cooperates, and in his cooperation he also believes, although perhaps unconsciously.

Healings have been performed for people in comas, or at great distances, who could not have known they were the subjects of prayer. But the flagging spirit of life in them was revived and stirred into action by the energy of Divine Mind focused by the person who prayed; and there was agreement in the healing process. The mysteries of the mind are deep and subtle, which is the reason healings through prayer appear miraculous.

The Christ Mind, where our authority lies, is the seat of love and creativity and all other qualities of God. It presents an amorphous, mysterious, perhaps even frightening aspect to our mortal minds. We revere the Christ Mind, perhaps love it, but few among us understand it. This, no doubt, is part of the reason for widely varying results from prayer. We do not know how to approach the Christ Mind, but in times of great stress or danger we cry out with heightened intensity, and often our need is answered swiftly because we have fulfilled the requirements of prayer. The earnestness of our prayers and the singleness of our minds, along with faith, rush the answer to us. Paul said: . . . *let your requests be made known to God.* (Phil. 4:6) It is also important that our requests be made known clearly to ourselves. God already knows them. If our minds are not clear about what we are praying for, the results are likely to be unclear. We are told that the spoken word of prayer brings manifestation. There is a reason for phrasing it this way. Some of us are lazy-minded, and if we simply let our prayer requests amble about in our minds, they may not focus sufficiently to define what we are seeking. When we speak the words, preferably aloud, we must first think them out and set them in phrasing that is distinctly descriptive. *"Speak the word"* we are told, which is a way of saying you should know what you want and make your request known.

This is not to say that nothing good ever comes to us unless we ask for it specifically. Many things come to us, seeming miracles, about which we have had no specific consideration. But as I previously pointed out, if we have a prayerful attitude, Divine Mind fills a need when it appears, perhaps even when we are not aware that the need is imminent.

Prayer Reciprocates

It is a demonstrable Truth that when you pray for another's healing you also are healed. Just as when you pray for another's prosperity, abundance flows to you. When you pray that God's love and peace shall fall upon another whose life is in turmoil, you also come to feel a sense of tranquillity. Even if the other person shows no outer evidence of responding to your prayer, you do. This may seem to deny the assertion that prayers are most effective when they are specific and that sincere prayers spring forth speedily to do their work where you send them. When you pray, you lift your consciousness into an attitude of prayer, and in this you are in the Christ Mind. In this Mind, your prayer goes where you send it, and it spreads into your own body and affairs.

A consciousness filled with any quality is likely to manifest it. This rule operates positively and negatively. For example, if you dislike someone intensely and should be so unthinking as to wish that person misfortune, you will likely receive it yourself.

Prayer is a powerful do-it-yourself healing therapy. It does not cost, but it is by no means without price. It takes dedication and concentration on the healing power of the Christ Mind within you, as well as strong faith. One must take charge of one's mind so that no thought of fear can clog the clear path to healing. Fear weakens prayer and reduces its effectiveness. A disciplined mind marshals the healing forces in proper order and deploys them for quick victory. A disciplined mind is an understanding mind, a faith-filled mind, and a mind dedicated to perfect health. One who disciplines the mind and prays with faith and thanksgiving will see past the appearance of illness. Control of mind and emotion is the price one pays for successful prayer therapy.

Any disease can be healed by prayer. But in many instances specific diseases are not healed by prayer. Reconcile these facts, and you have the reason some persons declare that prayer does not work. It appears to them that prayer is not effectual with respect to sickness or prosperity or success in private or business relationships or, for that matter, in anything that calls for a response beyond the scope of customary human action. If it seemed to work, it was simply coincidental and would have come about anyway without prayer, they reason.

Yes, No, or Maybe

A great many people believe that when we pray to God He says yes, no, or maybe. This would mean that God decides in each instance whether the thing you ask for is good for you or whether it might be better to wait a while. This is an abridgment of the freedom He gave you in the beginning. This concept increases one's doubt when praying, and doubt is an enemy of the free flow of communication between our consciousness and the heart of God. It can be very discouraging to spend hours in prayer for a long-treasured dream while at the same time wondering whether God is shaking His head and deciding no or even maybe, or perhaps taking His time in making up His mind whether to go with you or against you. This concept of prayer also encourages pleading and cajoling in trying to influence God to decide in your favor.

I have wonderful friends who believe in this kind of prayer, and I love them, but I cannot agree with them. Of course, they don't agree with me either. God does decide, but He decides through our minds. We decide by using the mental and spiritual equipment God gave us.

Surely God would not be so whimsical as to hem and haw over yes, no, or maybe when we ask for fulfillment of a strong desire that, in Truth, He gave us. In the event you have misinterpreted your intuitive leading and desire something that is contrary to your potential, you are free to make your own mistakes and become educated thereby.

Some persons today, like many of Jesus' followers of 2,000 years ago, desire a king, spiritual or civil, who will rule with complete autocracy and make all their decisions. But we cannot be automatons. It is not in keeping with our divine nature, which is founded in freedom of Spirit. We are free to win and free to fail, free to make our own happiness, free to live, love, dare, and express; and because of the unrestricted Mind of God active within us as our motivating force, we would have it no other way. God is principle. God is law. He is divine love that works in and through all the formed universe and its parts, harmonizing, accentuating the good, and sustaining the original purpose which is the benefit of all. God is not an emotional king subject to whimsical opinions or favoritism. He does not mollycoddle some and bear down on others. He is impersonal as the law of mathematics is impersonal. God loves each of His creations with a great unquestioning love, seeing no sin and no failure, and casting no blame. We are His beloved children in whom He is well pleased. Our assurance that God is ever with us, guiding and sustaining us, is in the Truth that He is our Father who created us in love and in His image and likeness.

I pray, and it is comforting to know that the answer to my prayer comes to me through divine law and not through divine impulse. The law works with me and for me and always with unalterable precision. It is my part to learn to understand the law and to abide with it.

The Doctor in the House

When I pray for healing of my body, I know that the healing is in my own hands. God is not only willing but eager to heal. My hands are God's hands, and my mind is God's omnipotent Mind; and His understanding directs my thoughts into healing channels. The power of God flows through all and performs the healing. To the question, "Is there a doctor in the house?" you can always be assured that, so far as you are concerned, the answer is yes. You have the Great Physician within your body temple. He does not need to make house calls; He lives there. He is available in any emergency and fully able to handle any crisis. If each of us could develop the faith that would keep us well, we would fulfill

His purpose in us. This is the best therapy. Physicians and surgeons play an important part in helping to maintain the health of our nation, and God works through them. How much better it would be if we could remain in perfect health so that doctors would not need to work from patient to patient "putting out fires" as they seem to do.

It is neither fair nor sensible to say that any disease can be healed by anyone at any stage of his unfoldment. Some may fail to achieve healing even when praying frantically and long. Some have failed and say that prayer is not effective. Some will continue to fail while praying mightily for healing. This is relative to the fact that, given a problem in calculus, not everyone will get the right answer. Some persons have concluded that a small ailment can be healed by prayer but that a serious illness takes something different. Some diseases, they point out, cannot be healed even by medical science with all its modern technology. These are the so-called incurable diseases. This is a misnomer. Tuberculosis was once called incurable. So was smallpox, and so were many other diseases that are now rarely encountered. But illness persists and in some areas is increasing rapidly. Science has not yet found a cure for some dread diseases that are leading killers of humankind, although progress is being made. Doctors can control polio but they cannot yet cure psoriasis. In laboratories throughout the world, scientists are working steadily to find cures for all manner of diseases that now scourge us. Over the years they have come up with triumphs, and every success came because someone heard the wise and compassionate word of God through intuition.

The Truth of the Matter

The Truth is that any disease can be healed by the prayer of faith. I am not referring to formalized and esoteric incantations that are known only to the initiated. I am referring to the prayer of perfect faith.

Jesus promised us that we can do the things He did and greater things. If we do not believe it, that is our problem. We must learn to pray as Jesus prayed. This means that we must change our minds from weakness and fear to pure faith. The fact that we have contracted a disease is an indication that we need to alter our habitual thoughts. If we have an illness that has not yielded to prayer, we are praying amiss. We need to change our approach. If we are under a doctor's care and a cure is not forthcoming, we need to change *our minds*.

If everyone understood how Jesus prayed, there would be no sickness. There also would be no wars, no inharmony, no unemployment, and no inflation. Changing our minds to the likeness of the Christ Mind means discarding a lifetime of false concepts based on imperfect interpretations of God and replacing them with new beliefs, some of which are difficult to accept in our present states of unfoldment. We need to cleanse our minds of the last vestiges of the seven Devils mentioned in an earlier chapter in this book. We must rid ourselves of belief that healing can be impossible. We must stop expecting and accepting sickness as a normal and inevitable way of life. Also, we need to replace condemnation of ourselves and others with the total and uncompromising love of Jesus Christ for all humankind. This is the hardest task of all.

We must believe in God, believe in prayer, and believe that any illness can do nothing other than yield to the power of the Christ Mind. We must accept that the natural condition of one's body is health and that one's body is constantly renewing itself to its original state. Let us know that God never wills illness in any form. For our own good, we need to establish new habits of thinking. To form better habits of mind action, we need to have affirmative ideas, ideas of love and faith, and we need to deny all error. These are Jesus Christ ideas.

We need not go all the way to perfection before we can begin to heal. Every man and woman alive is on the way toward God. Some have gained a greater understanding than others, but everyone is drawn irresistibly toward manifestation of divine qualities and the expression of divine potential.

You can heal yourself now. You have healed yourself of ailments in the past, and this ought to give you confidence to continue. Not only can you heal yourself of sicknesses but you can permanently rid your mind and body of acceptance of sickness. Because of a stubborn tendency to hang on to false states of consciousness, our progress toward emerging into the Christ Mind sometimes is slow, but we can use what we have learned as we go. We are knowledgeable apprentices.

An old saying goes, "The wheel that hollers gets the grease." At the same time, the rest of the wagon may be in imminent danger of collapsing. Any disaffection in your body cries to be healed, but it has a cause, and it is the cause that needs to be treated. Do not pray only for healing of a headache; pray to heal the worry or stress or whatever caused the headache. Do not heal the symptoms as doctors do; heal the cause which is in your consciousness. Heal your consciousness by replacing negative attitudes with positive beliefs and you will have automatically removed the cause as well as the symptoms of illness. To say that you attract sickness by your attitude may seem a harsh indictment, but you must accept it. All of us draw to ourselves negative responses that result from error thinking, but let us cast no blame either on ourselves or others. But we should come to understand the process through which unwanted reactions appear in our bodies and affairs. With that essential understanding, we can take productive steps to eliminate the causes that brought about the malfunction. The marvelous part is that when you have permanently eliminated the cause, you also have done away with all symptoms. Heal as you go. Do not wait until you think you are in the Christ consciousness. Jesus Christ grew in *"wisdom and stature."* He was thirty years old when He performed His first miracle. You are in training as He was, and the more you practice the healing consciousness the more proficient you will become.

Every healing ever accomplished came about because someone believed, the healer or the patient or both. Faith oils the machinery of prayer and causes it to run smoothly and productively. Without faith, good was never accomplished either in healing or in any other phase of living. Build your faith through study, meditation, prayer, and practice.

We are long accustomed to evidence of healing. Everyone has been healed of a variety of illnesses, and "ordinary" healings pass without notice. Healings have become notable only when they fall into the category of the miraculous. Every healing is a miracle in that it is "an event deviating from the known laws of nature, or transcending our knowledge of those laws" as defined in the dictionary. No one knows what happens during healing when the cells of the body readjust themselves and function again in their natural manner. When you heal your cold, you have performed a miracle; and if you can perform one you can accomplish others. The difference is that the "others" may seem more serious and frighten you. They simply take more faith, a stronger consciousness of health.

Pray for your healing, but pray in faith. Pray for the healing of your brother and you also will be healed. The miracle-working power of the Christ heals you right where you are in consciousness. As you grow in wisdom, the healing blessing of God flows more strongly through you. Healings will no longer seem miraculous.

I Hope, I Hope, I Hope

Alexander Pope wrote: *Hope springs eternal in the human breast,* and thereby idealized a common failing of the human mind. Referring to the dictionary, we find the prosaic meaning that hope is *a desire of obtaining or the promise that something desired will come.* Hope is comforting; it is a pleasant indulgence. Like daydreaming, it enables worried minds to endure themselves. Hope helps to pass the time, but that is all it does. Hope is of the future. It calls for manifestation of desires at some future time. Because of the power of mind action, that is when the manifestation is scheduled to come, at some time beyond the now. This is the time that never arrives.

Hope and *wish* are kindred words. Both are

passive, inert, with an interweaving of fear. Both can have a meaning in the present, but by far the greater usage is for some indeterminate time. You hope that something will occur or you wish that a certain thing would come to pass, sometime. Not now, but sometime. People are forever hoping that this or that nice thing will happen to them. The very concept behind the process of hoping pushes the consummation into the future. So such people hope all their lives, sometimes for the same thing. Some appear unable to give up hoping, even after a lifetime of failure to get what they hope for. This is an indication that they recognize a strong urge for accomplishment but misinterpret the means of accomplishing. Their feeble probing for happiness is doomed before it begins.

Mind Is Decisive

Hoping is not the way of the mind. The mind is naturally decisive. It is firm, scheduled for accomplishment. It does not know what to do with vague commands that do not prescribe action except perhaps at some undisclosed future time. It is not being asked to perform an act now, so it cannot. Nothing happens, ever. Your mind obeys no commands other than yours, and it does not obey even yours unless the instructions are definite. We think of daydreaming as occasionally resulting in manifestation, but that happens only when the air castle becomes real in one's mind and arouses a decree for its immediate manifestation. Hoping in its inconclusive nature is similar to ordinary, half-asleep daydreaming.

If you hope that you will awaken at 5 a.m. tomorrow, you have no assurance that you will, unless you have previously formed the habit of getting up at that hour. If you focus on the decree that you will awaken at five, you have more assurance that your mental alarm will go off. That is the difference. A decree gives your mind work to do, while hope tells it to go back to sleep for a while. Hope prohibits decisive action.

This is not to be a psychological or psychiatric treatise on motivation of the mind but, instead, a discussion of the promise and activity of prayer. We should know something of the mental processes and the catalysts that trigger them into activity. We should understand the direct interrelationship between one's thinking and the dynamic energy of prayer. Because the subconscious and conscious phases of mind are so embroiled with a multitude of things, any idea that is to be acted upon must be projected unequivocably upon the screen of mind.

Hoping will not do. Wishing will not do. Daydreaming has value, but not in bringing the creative power of mind to bear on manifestation. Casual contemplation without decision will not do. If you want action, you will have to decree action. A strong desire for immediate manifestation is a command for action. A hope for a future manifestation is a demand for inaction at the present. If for some good reason you must postpone a desire, yet want to keep it working on the back burner until an appropriate time this summer, let us say, do not hope it will come about in the summer; instead, decree the manifestation for August 1, or whatever date you desire, and state the year. Then hold to the thought of the date you have set.

This is one of the most common causes of failure in prayer—seeing a fuzzy, amorphous image of the desired result without perspective as to time and place. The activity of God is instantaneous and does not require time for preparation or manufacture. It happens now.

We know the good that God has for us already exists, awaiting our call to move it into actuality. Why put it off, even until next week, if you want it now? Certainly not until next month, next year, or some vague time in the future. Let us not hope for our good; let us decree it to be ours at this moment. When you pray for guidance or love or peace or for something material, hoping is a weak approach and reveals a mind that is uncertain and insecure and, by any definition, indecisive. If you have hoped for something for years, you have demonstrated that you do not know what you want but simply think it might be nice to have or be something like that. This is not the way to get it.

If all the hopes of humankind were laid end to end, they would make a very long string of probably pleasant but unfulfilled desires, a sad row of potential good. If you would be about your Father's business, you need to perform, to accomplish, to work toward your potential, both spiritual and material. God gave you a body with which to move about, a tongue with which to communicate, a mind to direct your whole activity and to hold your wants within a prescribed boundary of your developed destiny. Also, He gave you His

Spirit as your personal identity and passport into the world of accomplishment which you are to build on Earth. Prayer is your line of communication direct to your Source. The desires for which you pray are marks on the chart showing the extent of your progress toward your potential. Each answered prayer produces desires for greater accomplishment as well as progress toward your ultimate goal. If your prayers are not fulfilled, you are stymied, hoping for a demonstration that never comes. Your hope becomes self-deception. You credit yourself smugly with making great plans, and you hope. It is cruel deception. You, of course, believe it yourself and continue to be disappointed that the demonstration does not come. But you are not taking your life in hand and deciding to do something worthwhile with it. You are floating to nowhere on a quiet and pleasant stream of wishful thinking.

Don't hope, decree! Don't wish, accept!

Perhaps I am being too harsh. But if this scenario includes even a minor character trait or tendency that you recognize, let it bump you back into the path of your good. It is important, very important, that you do not deceive yourself. There is a world of difference—the difference between attaining your goal and missing the target entirely. Pray with confidence and conviction for a manifestation. Issue a decree that will roll back the iron gates of your mind prison and fulfill God's purpose for you.

Hoping or wishful thinking may fly into bizarre fantasies that find their outlet in daydreaming. Everyone daydreams. Studies show that people daydream up to twenty-five percent of their time. Contrary to popular opinion, daydreams are not all bad. They are not recommended, but some have side effects that could possibly be helpful in a number of ways, such as building self-esteem, relieving tension, getting rid of anger or fear, or even helping to develop a consciousness of success. After all, daydreaming is simply exercising your natural imagination and can have certain good effects as well as bad. Athletes, for example, increase their skills by imagining themselves winning in competition. Daydreaming at times may give your imagination a needed workout, stabilize your self-image, provide skills training, or take your mind off worries.

The problem with daydreaming is that it may cause people to spend their lives hoping for a manifestation that never comes. It can be a debilitating and useless waste of time. This kind of daydreaming never produces good and leads to disappointment and, finally, resignation.

There are those who say that hoping serves a good purpose in that it lifts one's mind to a higher level of pleasurable contemplation of happy events and expectation of joy. But hoping is not expectancy; it is pure wishing and has the effect of prohibiting one's good from approaching.

Jesus Christ did not say, "I hope I can raise Lazarus" or "I hope I can heal these lepers" or "I hope I can rise after three days in the tomb." When you hope, you are afraid you can't. When you decree, you know you can. We learned long ago that the mind is a manufacturing plant and thoughts are the machinery. We need good machinery to produce quality products rather than discards. Benjamin Franklin said, "He who lives upon hope will die fasting."

Some people indulge in hoping while clutching their rabbit's foot in one hand and an amulet in the other. The word *hope* is frequently used like an incantation, a magical shield against foul luck in the same manner as crossing one's fingers. "If it doesn't rain, I'm taking my wife and kids to the country this weekend," one says, and follows with "I hope." You know that person has no conclusive expectation of going to the country. He no doubt would like to go but fears that something is going to work against him. This is not the kind of thinking that should be associated with our desires and plans.

Jesus, speaking to the Pharisees, said: *"I tell you, on the day of judgment men will render account for every careless word they utter; for by your words you will be justified, and by your words you will be condemned."* (Matt. 12:36, 37) Words are the emissaries of the mind. Behind every word is an idea, and within every idea is the creative power of the one Mind, Divine Mind. It is the divine nature of every idea to be self-manifesting, to reproduce itself in like form. Idea, thought, word, is the natural sequence of expression. The creativity originating in the divine Source behind the idea carries through to the manifestation. Thoughts are things, Charles Fillmore said. They are entities filled with the power to shape, to form, to produce in accordance with their own nature. They must manifest themselves; they can do no other. The quality of creativity is never static but always evolving. It is ever working toward its inevitable conclusion that is the ultimate manifestation of the idea in which it finds itself cast.

Words Have Power

You start the evolution by entertaining the idea; only you can stop the process, and you do it by discarding or watering down the thought. If you allow the thought or idea to remain in your consciousness, it builds itself into a habit pattern which adds to its power of reproduction because it is not then subject to interruption or conflicting forces. Beware of negative habits of thought. They will cause you to continue to react negatively to circumstances and, thus, draw negation that you do not want into your life. What are words but crystallized thought? As such they have a greater cutting power than the original thought or idea because they are thought-focused and sharply formed, the idea delineated. The creative essence is thus concentrated into its final form, ready for the manifestation it seeks and will accomplish, unless you destroy it by altering your thought.

From this it becomes clear that words have power, power to bring into your experience the idea behind them.

Within the boundaries of our being are myriad ideas, each working to accomplish its own destiny. This has been going on all our lives in greater or lesser intensity, which accounts for the varying experiences we have encountered about a variety of things. We are still encountering them, good and bad, along with not-so-good and not-so-bad. We hold in our minds many ideas and conceptions about many things, and each of these ideas is working to make itself a fact in our lives. If true and positive and beautiful concepts predominate in our minds, our lives show it. But if negative reactions prevail, the shape of our lives will reveal that too.

You are obliged to accept the responsibility as well as the benefits of the enormous, nearly illimitable power of your consciousness. Your thinking faculty is the creative, formulating activity of Divine Mind individualized in you. As such it is your servant or your master, depending on the direction you give it. Thoughts and ideas are the product of divine, dynamic energy, and they make your world. You have a responsibility to your Creator, to yourself, and to the world in which you were sent to live, to use your creative capabilities to produce results leading to attainment of your divine potential. This has to be the purpose underlying the gift of creativity with which you were blessed in the beginning.

Choose your thoughts well. On that choice depends the tenor of your life. You choose the words representing your thoughts, and they are alive with creativity, carrying out the dictates of your consciousness. If you choose to speak positive words of faith, love, abundance, life, and harmony, you will justify your being and portray in your life the good that is integrated in the sequential creativity of thinking—thought, idea, and word. But if you choose to go the way of negation and speak words of inharmony, fear, disbelief, sickness, and lack, think not that you can receive benefits of the creative gift. The gift works with equal strength to produce hardship in your affairs. Let us mean what we say. When we want good, let us speak only good words. It is our consciousness, our habit thought, that sets the pace and form of our lives. We can and do sometimes selfishly speak at variance with our normal course of thought when we believe the words we say will serve us profitably although they do not represent our true attitude. Such false words will not create good, because in our hearts we know they are false, even if no one else does.

Words like *hope* spoken in doubt will not produce the desired result, because the inhibiting thought they engender does not call for manifestation. The tragic part of it is that people continue to express a doubting hope in the delusion that somehow good will come out of it in spite of their disbelief. Likewise, words such as *maybe* tend to spring from a hesitancy to take a bold stand, a positive stand, and a timid need for an "out" in case of failure. The expression "God willing" is another hedge against embarrassment in the event one's plans do not materialize as desired. This is a delusion. The Truth is that God is always willing to fill our arms with treasure when we extend them to receive. Because of imperfect semantics we are able to hide behind double-meaning words, sometimes without intent, and make statements that deep in our consciousness we do not mean or believe. Our true intent in the words we speak is the factor that gives them power and direction. What we really mean rather than what we say is fundamental in the formulating power of our speech. If we make a bold and positive-sounding statement but do not believe it, the statement is nullified.

The deep thoughts and attitudes that constitute our consciousness also make our environment. If your world is not all that you would like it to be, there is only one way to bring it into alignment with your divine potential of beauty, peace, and satisfying accomplishment. It is by changing the nature of your consciousness. This is done by prayer. In prayer you instill spiritual ideas of strength, faith, love, health, and abundance in your mind. There they become your attitude toward people and circumstances and all else that concerns you. Pray to God, laying your need before Him, and listen to His response, which comes to you through your intuition. Persistent meditation on ideas of Truth activate the dynamic energy of the Christ Mind which embodies the attributes and qualities of God. Your faith accepts the ideas required by your need to make you a whole and successful child of God.

Prayer brings God-Mind into your consciousness. Prayer is not only meditation, which is primary prayer, but it is also the good, positive, and prayerful thoughts you hold all day. Paul said: *Pray without ceasing,* which is a beautiul way to form your thoughts and words, and thereby your life, into a pattern of delight.

The Center of Things

Do you sometimes wish that you could just once be the center of things? Or does the very thought of being the center of things cause you to shudder or perspire? Being the center of things is a mixed blessing; it carries with it certain prestige, perhaps some ego gratification, an opportunity to demonstrate your talents, and a chance to be heard; but on the other hand, it represents responsibility.

Being the center of things is a heady experience. The person who occupies that position is the leader; he sets the pace and direction. It is an important position. To some introverted people, it is frightening.

But whether you like it or not, you are the center of things. You are the center of *your* world, not *the* world. Everything in your world follows you, depends on you, obeys you. You are in control of all the organs and cells of your body, your health, your finances, your degree of success and well-being, your social relationships, and the state of your consciousness. And that ought to be enough for anyone's ego.

Though you are the center of things in all that concerns you, you also have a responsibility to all the components of your world, to lead them into harmonious interrelationships that allow full and joyous expression for all. This is a grave responsibility because you have the power to upset the equilibrium at any time and to cause others to suffer. Other people, also in their private worlds, can and do affect you. This is good when their effect is pleasant and helpful. But if dissension arises, there ensues a war of the worlds in which the balance of each is disturbed and everyone suffers.

There ought to be harmony in God's world. But harmony depends on the presence or lack of harmony in the heart of the center of things in the personal world. The harmony in your personal affairs, which is your world, depends on the harmony in your heart. Harmony in your soul reflects itself into harmony in your expression of life, and such harmony is a developed quality. Harmony in your world, as in music, means agreement between components and blending of disparate segments into a smoothly flowing whole. Harmony, as in everything else in your world, has its source in the action of your mind. To restore lost harmony may take a sublimation of certain belligerent tendencies of consciousness or corralling of perverse concepts, but there is no other way than through deliberate action of mind. Accept your role as the center of things and eliminate the belief that you are necessarily compelled by circumstances.

You Are in Charge

Your divine gift of dominion means that you are in complete charge of your world. This may come as a shock to timid souls observing their crutches being snatched. But you do not have to walk alone. You are the center of things, but you are not indivisible. The center of things within you is God, and no further division can be made. God is One. God is One with many attributes and qualities, but each attribute contains all the others. John wrote: ... *God is love*. (I John

4:8) It is God as love who stirs up the desire for peace in your heart. Love is the guiding influence that spreads balm on troubled areas of your world, whether it is malfunction in your body, rebellion in your mind, or stumbling in your affairs. Love heals all problems. So we arrive at the Truth that God's love working through you is the center of things in your world.

Love is an all-inclusive quality spreading into countless areas. Your expressions of love can be toward members of the opposite sex, chocolate, sailing, gardening, friends, winter, summer, the feel of success, the appearance of good, God, or anything that arouses a strong emotional attraction. Love is a power of the first magnitude. It binds, heals, builds, homogenizes. Love is the center of things not only in your world but in the private world of all other persons, and is the common denominator that draws them together into the interdependent mass that is humankind. Love is good; it is benign; it wants only to express in everyone and everything and every relationship. It expresses through you a thousand times a day in things you do and think, and it is responsible for the good you express and that which is expressed to you.

You can do no better than to magnify this divine quality in all that you do, think, and say. There is never a short supply. You cannot give it all away. Like a smile, it rushes back to bless you.

In Corinthians Paul wrote: *And if I have prophetic powers, and understand all mysteries and all knowledge, and if I have all faith, so as to remove mountains, but have not love, I am nothing.* (I Cor. 13:2) Later, he said: *So faith, hope, love abide, these three; but the greatest of these is love.* (I Cor. 13:13) There are few words, including God, that appear more frequently in the Bible than the word love. And there is none other than God that carries greater significance in the lives of people.

People have become more eclectic as well as unrestrained in their expression of emotions than in the past. The word love appears in conversation and print more frequently. When I was a boy, one rarely heard the word in ordinary conversation. I was raised in a family in which emotions were restrained. I do not recall ever hearing my father speak the word love. He must have, for he was a kindly man. But he did not speak it in my presence. He would not have said, "I'd love to go fishing." He would have said, "Come on, let's go fishing," but never, "Wouldn't you love to go fishing?" I'm sure that if I had gone around the house saying that I love to do this or I'd love to do that, the rest of the family would have looked at me strangely and perhaps with some concern. Now I love to say that I love this or I would love to go here or there, including fishing.

Love the Good

Love is a quality of being and of mind that all of us should cultivate assiduously. It is a quality that sustains. There are many kinds of love, or different interpretations of it, but all are from the same Source. There are passionate love, mother love, love of self, love among persons, representing an extended degree of friendliness, love of power and job and success and nature and adventure and travel and home. You could spend the day adding to the list. We all have happy emotions toward many things, and this can be called love. Love sees no evil or error. Love sees good. Where love sees good, good appears. Love is never angry, never disheartened, although we who love may sometimes be both; but a contemplation of love will take us back to the happy emotion.

If you allow love to hold sway in your heart, you will never lack self-esteem, because you will love the good that is in you. You will love the good in other persons and in situations, and if there seems to be no good in them, you will find it. Where you see it, it appears. Love in your mind gives you a good perspective of the world. It makes you understanding of others and compassionate, but it does not insist that you compromise your ideals. Instead, it strengthens your character and makes you stand firm against its erosion. Love is the universal quality that finds its echo everywhere. Love your job, and it seems to love you; love your neighbor, and he will be good to you; love yourself, and you will not let yourself down; love good, and good will envelop you. You can be safe with love.

It is difficult to imagine a world without love. What a stark and empty place it would be! Francis Bacon described a similar effect in an essay written about 1600: *A crowd is not company, and faces are but a gallery of pictures, and talk but as tinkling cymbals, where there is no love.* Love between the sexes has been a popular subject for novelists since the earliest writers penned their works on parchment. And it has been equally popular with nonfiction writers and essayists and even scientists who have poked, prodded, dissected, and analyzed it down to the last sigh. The Bible is full of it. Love is a major concern of all people. Psychiatrists tell us that love is essential to a balanced nature, and lack of it can result in serious aberrations in both men and women. Lack of love may make a criminal. Nothing makes one feel so alone as to feel unloved. But this is primarily love among people, one for another.

There are other expressions of love equally important to our stability and general wellbeing. Love of God is primary, because love of God means love of good, which is the basis of all endeavor to improve one's relationships, health, and condition of life. Love is a powerful motivating force for good. Love of health, not fear of ill-health, is normally the motivation for the strenuous regimens people frequently keep to regain health or to maintain it. Love of success, not love of money, is the prime motivation for a lifetime of hard effort men and women exert to attain to high places in business or the professions. You were born with love as an integral part of your being, and it has remained with you as your vision of completeness. Love takes the positive view; love within you loves good, so you love good. Love loves to excel, because to excel is better than to fail. Love loves a healthy body, because a healthy body expresses a divine ideal. Love does not hate evil, because love cannot hate. When people hate, their whole beings are poisoned and they reveal sickness in mind, body, and affairs. Love then struggles to urge them back to normalcy. And until they change their consciousness, they experience a sense of intense guilt.

If you do not love someone or something, you are incomplete, and your emotional nature will never let you forget it. You cannot be happy, because love is the happy emotion; but you yearn to be happy. Love is very much a part of life. It is essential to well-being and must be nurtured and treasured; it is a pearl of great price.

Release Love

If one feels unloved and seems not to love anyone or anything, one feels a great lack, a painful feeling. This is an indication that he or she at least has a love of loving. Love is alive within all, desiring expression. You are capable of loving. Release love and it will burgeon into beauty and joy, and you will again feel whole. You need more than a passing fancy or a casual attraction; you need a great love, a love that fires your mind and enthralls your emotions. It can but need not be love for a person; it can be any love that totally absorbs your mind and thrills you to exultation. If nothing else, try painting or writing or floriculture or ceramics. You have always known what you would most like to do; you have felt the gnawing urge all your life. Whatever it is pursue it and love it, and the pursuit will make you happy. No one can lay out a program for you; it is a private matter. One can only say that without someone or something to love, the world becomes dull and barren. People appear to be faceless stick figures moving like automatons until you invite love into your life.

Of all the attributes and qualities of God, love is without doubt the most easily recognizable as such. Consciously possessing it gives one a warm, exultant feeling, a sense that all is right with the world. The more you love, the more beautiful all things appear.

Love your work; love your family; love yourself; love your neighbor; love something or someone with all your heart. Love humankind. You need not condone the injustice or error you see about you. Simply realize that it has always been with us and will continue to be until all people come to follow the admonition of Jesus to *"love your neighbor as yourself."*

Meanwhile, love the good that you see wherever you find it, and leave the bad. Look for the good in every situation and you will ultimately see it grow, spread, and flow to you in greater measure than ever before. Always look for the good. Do not accept the accusation that you are unrealistic or deluding yourself. On the contrary, there is nothing more real than good. And by identifying yourself with it wherever it may be, you are performing an act of love which itself is divine. You have a responsibility to express the love in your heart because that expression enriches you and your environment in a way nothing else can.

As the center of things in your world, you are answerable for its well-being. It is your place to take care of it, nurture it, and bless it. Look for good in unlikely places, for you never know where you will find treasures to glorify your world. Treasures such as companionship, joy, health, abundance, success, understanding, faith, love, and material good are yours for the finding. And the greatest of these is love.

Pray for your world first, and then pray for the outer world. Pray not from a sense of selfishness but to cleanse yourself so that you are prepared to pray for others. Pray that love will come into your world in great abundance, bringing its balm and blessings so that you may serve as a booster station and send love forth multiplied into the private worlds of those about you. This is not a fanciful or visionary concept. It is pragmatic. As you give, you receive in equal measure.

Prayer and love are closely akin. Prayer is an act of love for God and for the consummation for which you pray. Make sure you always pray in love. Do not pray in fear and doubt, and certainly not in condemnation of yourself or your neighbor. Pray in faith. When you pray without faith you do not reach God, because you have set up an impassable block. Pray in love by holding in mind the best that you can conceive, the highest manifestation of your highest desire, so that you downgrade neither your desire nor yourself. Pray in love by expecting God to answer your prayer, giving Him credit for capability and willingness. Pray as the center of things, and love will become your servant, alert to fulfill every wish of your heart. Without thought of selfishness, but with a desire to serve yourself and the outer world in equal measure, pray that love will be established everywhere in the fullness of its benign power. The presence of love is the presence of dynamic energy. And the expression of love is the irresistible but gentle movement of the blessings of God.

A Universal Need

Above all, you have a need for love. You and everyone else. This is why you seek it, why you seek ever more of it. You have a congenital need not only to receive love but to express it. Love is the universal need and a universal inspiration. By its own dynamic benevolence, love inspires all people to perform great acts, heroic acts of unaccustomed splendor. Love inspires greater works than one seems capable of, greater heights of attainment than one can perceive.

Inspiration means breathing in, as expiration means breathing out. In the soul's progress toward perfection, inspiration is breathing in, or taking on, God's pure love and wisdom. It is a miracle of communication through our intuitive nature by which God sends His instructions or guidance. Breath is life. The breath of God is the life of God flowing through our being, and it includes not only life but love and energy and all the faculties of the Most High. In paeans of praise, Job cried: *"The spirit of God has made me, and the breath of the Almighty gives me life."* (Job 33:4) This inspiration of God came upon this man of the Old Testament and brought him out of suffering and degradation into the pure light of understanding, a new life of power and affluence and order twice as great as he had before.

The breath of the Almighty continues to flow in prayer to all humankind, leading us *beside still waters* and on the broad path of righteousness toward our divinely appointed destiny of at-one-ment with Him. In this closeness is the release of struggle, failure, and sorrow, and emergence into the body of God, which is the ordained heaven on Earth, shedding a glorious light in which is the attainment of every good desire.

We are the center of things, and the center of us is God's love. Through His love we are healed and prospered and blessed. We need never beg for God's love; it has always been ours, a built-in gift from our Father and Creator. Knowing this, we can follow the voice of our intuition with complete assurance that it is divine guidance and must lead us to our highest good. We need only check our interpretation of intuition's message to make sure our human consciousness and will have not bent it to our personal demands. We see only the temporary advantage; God sees the rest of our lives. We will see as God sees when we pray and meditate until the voice of intuition comes through clearly and positively with no lingering hint of questioning. If the guidance of intuition should seem to weaken, do not release it until you have made certain it is not fright or awe at the prospect of what the guidance might mean in responsibility that is influencing you to shrink from its divine edict. Give your intuition the benefit of the doubt; it is your line of communication direct to God-Mind in which there is no error.

God, love, inspiration, and you are the center of things. Let the natural flow to you from the other members of this executive council be smooth and unimpeded, and your world will be justified, prosperous, and happy.

Say Yes

The primary goal of humankind is happiness; but before we can achieve happiness, we must say yes to happiness. Before we can be prosperous, we must say yes to prosperity. Before we can be healed, we must say yes to healing. The trouble is, we say no much of the time.

Happiness, healing, and abundance are products of our mental processes, working under the authority and direction of Divine Mind. There is one unnamed and sometimes unrecognized ingredient that can stop the whole process, and that is consent. Our minds must consent to cooperate and be used.

You may consider this statement laughable. Of course you want happiness. Of course you want prosperity and health and other good things. Who doesn't? So what is this about consent? Let me answer by reminding you that you already have all you will ever need or want, and always have had through the love of God for His creation. May I remind you also that demonstrations of good come by means of mind energy working through your consciousness, calling your desires into actuality. It becomes clear, then, that if your life does not display evidence of manifestation of the gifts of God that are within you, the stoppage must be in the failure of your mind to do its part. Your mind has withheld its consent.

The paradox is not easily understood. The reasons are because of stubborn and habitual negative thinking involving falsehoods and misconceptions. Some persons may refuse to accept this by claiming it is ridiculous to accuse them of not wanting something they feel they want very much. I am not saying they do not want it, but I am saying they have refused to accept it. Your consent is an absolute prerequisite to any manifestation in your life, good or bad. We have become accustomed to the idea that our minds are not only seats of all desire; they are the dynamic energy that molds it, images it, and finally draws it out into formulated manifestation. But perhaps it comes as a bit of a surprise that our minds are also culprits that bar the formulation in spite of continuing to be the reservoirs of desire for its manifestation.

Why Do We Doubt?

Why do we stand in the way of our own good? We do not realize it, of course, although at times we perhaps have an inkling of it. When we set for ourselves high goals that frighten us by their elevation and scope, we may delude ourselves that we are clinging stubbornly to those goals while under the surface we are plagued by a gnawing doubt that we cannot reach them or cope with them after we have attained them. This is a common happening that besets many of us and dilutes our resolve. Thus, our minds withhold their full consent.

A young girl desires to be an actress. Acting sounds glamorous to her. She may have talent, but she makes no real effort to accomplish her goal. She doesn't know how to go about it, and her timidity and doubting mind restrain her from finding out. Maybe it is the voice of reason telling her it is a silly idea.

Perhaps not. In any event, she continues to daydream. A young man working in a factory has a strong desire to be a surgeon; but when he considers the years of university study and internship and setting up a practice, he gives up and carries all his life the desire to be a surgeon. Later he will become embittered by his failure to spend the necessary years preparing for what he is convinced would have been a spectacular career.

Why do so many men and women imbued with exciting ideas of accomplishment hold back their consent? Do they distrust their intuition? Are they super-cautious and decide to wait and see? Do they not know that every strong hunch of good quality comes from Divine Mind and that God is prepared to smooth their way if they will but start? Are they frightened at the prospect of stepping out on a new road, or are they simply lazy? Whatever the reason, it is an unfortunate fact that many powerful ideas that would lead to one's happiness and success never get off the ground. Someone's mind lacked the fortitude to say yes.

How many ideas have you and I had and thought, "Wouldn't that be wonderful!" but let them die because they would take time and effort? Besides, we were getting by all right without them.

When we have a need, we receive a barrage of ideas. If we do not consent to certain ideas, no one else will. No one else can. There is a good chance, however, that someone else will use our ideas to great benefit. You have seen it happen. Ideas of Divine Mind are available to everyone, and each of us takes what he needs and wants. We take what we need, but because of the lethargy of human nature we too often consent only to the easy ones and let the more difficult ones go by. Now and then we see a man or woman of strength and determination and perseverance who consents to an idea and carries it through to a successful conclusion gaining honor and riches. They are the leaders, the geniuses, the Nobel Prize winners, the millionaires. They are the extraordinary individuals to whom blessings seem to flow in unending abundance, all because their minds say yes.

We can paraphrase Rudyard Kipling's poem:

Oh, the years we waste and the tears we
waste
And the work of our head and hand

Belong to the mind that did not know
And now we know it never did know
And did not understand!

We are incredibly ignorant and stubborn
not to recognize the ideas that come through
our intuition. We ought to recognize them as
our lifeline to material salvation. We have
been told again and again, urged again and
again, and punished again and again, by our
unheeding refusal to accept our good. We can
no longer remain in ignorance. The experiences of our lives make it increasingly clear
that we must take control of our destinies.
We have allowed ourselves to be mishandled
by circumstances and to be denied our birth-
rights by outside forces. How much longer
can we stand by and see the torment of imperfect health, finances, and social relationships
continue without promise of relief? This is
not the way of Divine Mind, which envisions
no defeat nor halfhearted success. If you
would be in tune with your Creator as you
were meant to be, you must fulfill the potential of His creative power expressed in you.
That means an about-face for many of us. All
we need to confirm the dominion God gave us
is to consent and follow through.

Say Yes

Few among us are completely satisfied or unconditionally happy. We were not meant to be. We were born with divine discontent. The fires of creativity are ever stirring within us, singeing our lethargy, licking with a searing flame at our unbelief. It is an eternal flame of newness and greatness that never dies.

More to Come

Perhaps the world calls you a success, which means that you have consented many times to be used by this holy flame and have blazed new trails and profited thereby. But it is not over. It never will be over. There are greater heights before you than behind you. You who have shown yourselves ready to venture are destined to scale them. All your life the flame of creativity will open new vistas to you, unless and until you allow yourselves to become unadventurous and filled only with quiet dreams. Even then it is not over. Creativity and daring are still inherent within you, and in silent moments you sense that, like the inscription over the arch of an ancient Grecian temple, "There is yet more in you."

What is the real reason some men and

women stand above others in accomplishment? It is because they consent to be used by the creative force within them while others crawl into shells of fear, or laziness, or ignorance, and consistently say no. How do we know when we are being asked to say yes? No one can escape knowing. The requests, or opportunities, are hammered into our consciousness in response to our every need. They never let us forget them. Everywhere we go and in everything we do, we are reminded of the desire running deep in our being. Everywhere we go, opportunities are set in our paths to point out the way of expression. This is the work of the Christ Mind within us, drawing to itself the means and sustenance to attain its potential in us.

But suppose we misinterpret the call from deep within our minds and turn into the wrong path? We will have lost nothing except perhaps a little time, and we have enough of that in a lifetime. Meanwhile, we have obtained experience, sharpened our capabilities, and improved our perceptions. After discovering our mistake, we can spring forward with greater directness than before. But if you are doubtful about the meaning of a message your intuition has received, ask God to help you interpret it. The meditations of your heart establish communication and open your mind to receive the word of enlightenment from the Source of all wisdom. This is the proved method you always have used to find the answer to all problems, and it continues to serve. Go to God with an open mind and let His love fill you with an overwhelming conviction of the Truth, which is His way of making certain you understand.

How to Listen

When you enter into meditation, do so realizing that the answer you seek is of critical importance. Know that the true answer is sculptured to fit your talents, your capacities, and your faculty for perseverance and enthusiasm. It is fortunate for us that we need not seek among thousands of possibilities to find the secret goal that conforms in all ways with the needs and capacities of our nature. The wise and loving Father has arranged it so our private goal is presented to us as an intuitive idea, and we have the thrill of shaping, forming, and bringing it into full manifestation. As you proceed toward fulfillment of your potential, love yourself so that inhibition may be removed from your path. Let your love, unadulterated by fear, go out to bless others, and they in turn will bless you. Do not hate another person. In hate you see the same imperfections as in yourself, which tarnishes your perspective. Do not hate or even dislike yourself, because hatred is abrasive, and self-hatred is self-destructive.

Above all, do not be unduly influenced by outer pressures that could bind you, whether persons or circumstances, not even by books you read. Use others as guides or sounding boards, but stand firm against them as arbiters. Rely on your own indwelling wisdom, which is the true wisdom for you and is available at the instant you turn within to consult Spirit with unworried faith.

Let us joyously proclaim our agreement with the goal we have been charged to attain. It is that goal that makes life worthwhile, that provides the sublime happiness to which we were born. Our goal is made up of many goals interrelated and designed to conform to our nature. Our overall goal is the same as for all people, to know God and to draw close in perfect at-one-ment with Him who is the Christ in our hearts. We have other, private, objectives—to remain healthy, to enjoy abundance, to love and be loved, to see our families provided for, to attract friends, to be wholly happy, to all of which we must give our consent. And there are specific goals that have to do with means of earning a living, and of equal importance, to give ourselves a sense of accomplishment without which we cannot be content.

In Victorian-style novels, the late teens were prescribed as the age of consent, particularly for young women. The age of divine consent is any age, whenever one is called upon to face decisions. We consent to happiness, and we consent to disappointment. We consent to sickness, and we consent to health. We consent to anger, and we consent to peace. We consent to accept and implement messages received through our intuition, or we consent to willful disregard of them. Also, we consent to the consequences. Whatever comes into our lives must first have our consent. We seem not to consent to an accident or other catastrophe, but when the truth is known, we find that we have consented by the nature of our consciousness or habitual attitude. We consent to live, and we consent to die. We can refuse to consent as

when we deny evil, in which case we consent
to good.

Consent has several synonyms: acquiesce,
approve, concur, agree, permit, and acknowl-
edge. In all these are different shades of
meaning, but all mean to accept. We have
agreed to accept all that we consent to, and
we consent to everything that affects our
lives. We even consent to an irritable personality, and we agree to the boomerang results. We consent to loneliness, although
some might argue that, saying it is not their
fault they are alone and no one loves them.
Loneliness is a state of mind rather than an
absence of other persons with like interests.
One is never alone. Not only is there an indwelling God, there are books and hobbies
and beautiful outdoors and, all else failing,
one always has one's thoughts.

We not only consent to loneliness but even
inflict it upon ourselves. Releasing inordinate
shyness or self-centeredness or irritability,
and cultivating instead a genuine interest in
people and their pursuits, eliminates loneliness. But first we must consent to that, too.
Let us withdraw our consent from all negative things that pile depression upon us, and
substitute consent to the good and joyous

things the world has to offer. Our intuition will tell us what they are. Unhappiness is a contract to which you have put your seal through agreement. Unhappiness will fulfill its part of the contract to the letter, just as you will fulfill yours through your suffering.

Insight is akin to intuition. It is perception of the inner nature of things aside from their form. We have spiritual insight as an inherent part of our mental equipment. We use spiritual insight to evaluate not only the message of our intuition but also the messages coming through our senses. Insight is instinctive. Instinctively we recognize God as the Lord of our being, and our spiritual perception reveals the boundless extent of His love. All divine qualities work together for our good; and we are whole and complete even to the evaluating quality to distinguish right from wrong and good from bad. We know where to put our consent.

A Clean Slate

Before we can ever hope to rise out of limitation, we must cleanse our consciousness of not only the idea of limitation but other aberrant ideas as well. Go to God with a clean slate—without preconceived notions of what He does and does not want of you. Say simply: *Thy will be done.* And mean it. Then listen, and consent to your intuition as His messages of love and guidance flow into your mind. It is essential that you subdue your personal will, which no doubt has frequently pushed you into trouble, and ask that God's will be done. This will not result in loss of freedom, nor is it an indication of indecision. Instead, it will transform your life through your consent to right decisions in every circumstance. Some persons might feel they were giving up their rights, their integrity, the privilege of thinking for themselves, but this is not so. Entering into the will of God in your affairs reinforces your personal rights to which you are accustomed, strengthens your integrity, and at the same time rids you of the burden of wrong answers you have developed in your freedom of thinking. Deny all that is unlike the nature of God, and consent to all that is.

As we have long known, God is not only law-giver but Law itself, inexorable Law, Law that never fails. There is a law of mind action that takes its substance from and becomes divine law. This law ordains that whatever we hold in our minds shall manifest in our lives. It redounds to the marvelous benefit of humankind. The ideas that men and women meditate on and love and believe in will inevitably appear. Beauty in your heart becomes beauty in your life. Love, health, and abundance in your consciousness are expressed as love, health, and abundance in your body and affairs. When you consent to good, it is yours.

The law also says that when you consent to negative things such as sickness, lack of money, and bad social relationships, these things come to you. The law is impersonal and inexorable. Say no to all that you do not want in your life and it will avoid you. The law of consent works for everyone equally, like the law of gravity. Set up the conditions, and the law will follow through precisely, for you or against you. You can't beat it.

Thank God for Prayer

Thank God for prayer. What would we do without it? Some persons try to deny the efficacy of prayer and even the existence of God, but they are a defiant few. Neither God nor prayer need our defense. The fact that no one has ever seen God is not proof that He is not now controlling and sustaining the universe. There is much evidence of His presence. It would be well if we would now and then enumerate His works in our behalf in order to renew and reinforce our faith. But as for those who say there is no God, let us bless them and let them go. We need not be unduly concerned about their welfare, because God takes care of them anyway, to the full extent of their consent to the law.

It has been said, with truth, that God does

not need our prayers, but we do. We need constantly to correct our course, as the space scientist corrects the satellite's course to keep it on track.

Prayer is defined as communion with God. This is a skeletonized definition. Prayer also includes reverence and joy and release and love and expectation and faith. Along with it is God's response. His guidance may come as the still small voice or as a clap of thunder to assure us that our needs are even now being fulfilled. Prayer gives us comfort and confidence. It provides sure guidance and a sense of security. God fills our needs, more than we ask, in perfect ways that are designed for our consciousness and pattern of life. All this is prayer. We pray in terms of ideals; God answers in higher ideals. We ask from a limited consciousness; God gives from an unlimited supply all that we can accept.

There is nothing visionary or impractical about praying. It is as practical as wearing shoes in a briar patch. Prayer is your protection against all that would assail you. When you need guidance, or healing, or help with your finances, or comforting, or a tangible thing such as a job, or perhaps your need is simply for reassurance, it is supplied in prayer. There is no faster or surer way to attain your desires. Prayer is your open line to God, who is the giver of all gifts. Before you pray, while you are praying, after you pray, give thanks. Thanksgiving is good for your soul. It is important when you pray, because it attunes your consciousness to the wavelength of God and, on that wavelength, all good speeds to you. God is your one and only Source, and prayer is your contact with Him. Thank God for prayer!

Millions of people on Earth have needs and desires without number, and every need is of supreme importance to someone. In times of desperation, when our private wants remain unfulfilled, it may appear to us as individuals that we have been lost in the shuffle. It is comforting to realize that we do not contend with others for God's attention. We have His ear constantly, for He is within us. The Christ Mind, or I AM, is God at the center of our being. His sole purpose is to sustain us and guide our steps.

Guidance is not what some people believe they want. They think they want God to give them whatever they desire. God allows all persons complete freedom of decision, but He also gives us the privilege to contact Divine

Mind to receive the blessing of divine guidance. This guidance leads us up the straight path to our highest good. Yet, some persons willfully disregard the counsel that comes from their hearts and plunge blindly into impassable thickets and dead-end canyons, and over precipices, and declare that they are free.

There is perhaps no other goal so universally desired or earnestly sought as freedom. People spend much time scheming and laboring for what they believe will lead them to release from the yoke of circumstances, or ill health, or from other persons, and give them the freedom of action they desire. Many struggle in vain. It is futile to try to change conditions in your outer life while you hang on to old and inhibiting concepts within. Rid yourself of negative attitudes and beliefs, and negative conditions will die of starvation.

Believe that you are inferior to others and, in effect, you will be. Believe that the world conspires against you, and it will. Deep-seated beliefs that you are not really meant to be happy, or healthy, or prosperous may stubbornly refuse to give you freedom. You have, however, one powerful ally available to you, and that is divine understanding. It is gained through meditation and prayer. The false idea of lack of freedom stems from giving away control of one's mind to other persons and outer conditions. If you feel restrained or limited, you need to pray for an improved self-image, a self-image in which you view yourself as a spiritual being with a birthright of full dominion over your affairs. You can assert your authority, not with belligerence but with love, and live permanently in a state of self-control, which is the highest freedom to which you can aspire. Jesus said: "*... you will know the truth, and the truth will make you free.*" (John 8:32) The truth is that you are Spirit and are free with the freedom of Spirit. You are free in everything but your mind; and mind can make slaves and cowards of us all.

Our minds inevitably outpicture what we believe about ourselves and our world. One cannot hide one's habitual thinking. The effect is plain for all to see. You can look at me and tell whether I act with fear and doubt or with confidence. You know whether I have built a consciousness that accepts ill health and limitation or one that takes its authority from Divine Mind and permits only concepts of vibrant health and abundant prosperity. I am what I have allowed my thinking to make me.

A New Life

But we are blessed with the opportunity for prayer. We may pray any time, pray without ceasing, and God hears us. We have the privilege of building a new life through prayer. We accomplish it by holding in mind what we want to do or be and by carrying the concept to God in prayer. It serves no good purpose to plead with God for His gifts; when we are ready to receive, they will come to us. In joy and gratitude, we give thanks before we receive as well as afterward, especially before because this proves our faith.

We need prayer. We need God in every situation. It is not enough to say we will think ourselves into health, or abundance, or any other good. Our faith in ourselves quails before the specter of the world, and we are numbed; but the realization that we are not alone and friendless restores our courage. The mighty Spirit of God does His work through us, providing confidence and releasing our ability. Our brain is not our mind; our brain is simply a lump of matter forming an apparatus that can be made to think. Our mind takes its identity from Divine Mind and occupies space in every atom of our being. Mind pumps life into our bodies and ability to think into our brains, culminating in our consciousness, which represents the total effect of our mind activity. The creative authority in our thinking and the reservoir of power in our consciousness are not ours but God's, and we use them only because we were given that privilege at the time of our creation. It is a privilege that God never withdraws but is ours for all time. We are free to use divine creativity in any way we choose, but we must take responsibility for the effects of our choice.

We attune our consciousness to the love and will of God by deep meditation and prayer. Prayer is therapeutic as well as providing guidance and counsel; it recharges our minds and renews our bodies. Prayer is our contact with God and the "open sesame" to the riches of His kingdom.

We all know love as a divine principle that attracts and holds all good. In another form, it is also a universal need expressed as personal attachment among people. Not a man, woman, or child escapes a sense of emptiness when isolated from love. A natural bond of feeling exists among humankind that constantly requires reinforcement by appreciation or approval, along with experiencing the outflow of love within one's being. But great as is the need to give and receive affection, there is an infinitely greater need to feel the love of God. Love from another person bolsters our sense of worth, but the love of God is the source of our acceptance of the good that appears in our lives. Recognition of the unquestioning love of almighty Spirit gives us courage and faith to accept His blessings. Love of God comes into our consciousness through our intuition, and we know we are loved by the Lord of creation. Knowing this, who can think of himself as mean, or deprived, or unimportant? Some persons seem to consider themselves in that light and are lonely and embittered, but in reality they have crusted their inner vision with belief in their vulnerability to forces of the world. They, and everyone, need prayer to draw them into the circle of God's love. Meditating on the attributes and qualities and works of God will soothe the most embittered heart and restore a consciousness of divine love and peace, as well as a sure and exultant knowing that all is well.

We have discussed prayer from many viewpoints and have realized together that prayer is the most important element in our climb toward the highest expression of our inner selves. We have considered how to pray, and cleared away not only the mystique but also the widespread misinformation about what prayer is. Jesus Christ in His teaching did not separate favored from unfavored ones and say these may pray and those may not. His message was for all people. He told the multitudes to pray, and He gave them the Lord's Prayer, which begins, *"Our Father."* Everyone may pray; everyone can pray; everyone must pray. We have looked at prayer and have discerned the elemental factors that enter into its working processes. We have seen seeming miracles appear out of the invisible, and the unknowable become known because someone prayed. I hope I have not made prayer seem too easy.

Prayer is simple but not easy, uncomplicated but requires know-how and, certainly, practice. It is simple because it is neither more nor less than communion with God. It is not easy because it demands discipline and may require that you change your habitual thinking. It could mean that you have to build a whole new consciousness. Difficult or easy as it may be, prayer is your only hope of accomplishment.

Almost everyone prays, but hardly anyone gets consistently satisfying results. Some persons, in fact, pray all their lives and rarely receive what they desire. But "hope springs eternal." I have bad news for such people. So long as they continue to pray in the same old unknowing way, they will continue to get the same results.

To pray aright, you need a clean mind and heart. Clean in the sense of being uncluttered with fear. If you are going to pray doubting that God will give you what you ask, you are better off not to pray at all, because the repetition of your fears will impress the unwanted condition ever more firmly upon your life. That is the way with mind action. It is creative and inevitably reproduces the content of its thinking. You must know God as your loving Father, omnipotent, omniscient, omnipresent, so that His image of preeminence in your mind will arouse a conviction that He is able and willing to come to your aid. You must rid yourself of a sense of unworthiness, inferiority, weakness, or that you are past redemption. You must admit to yourself that you cannot do it alone and that you need the encouragement and help of God. Realize that the higher being you pray to is the Christ Mind which is part of your being and comprises all the power, love, creativity, health, and abundance of the universe.

Forgiveness Vital

Know that in the beginning you received the gift of dominion over your life through dominion over your thoughts, and bear this in mind when you pray. You must go to God with a heart free of condemnation. Forgive yourself of everything, and forgive everyone and everything. Go to prayer with no blame in your mind, only love. See the potential of perfection in you, now partly attained and the remainder attainable. Know that you are a spiritual being, a child of God with an inheritance of all that He is. Remember that this need of yours that looms so large and grave and portentous is a small matter in the eyes of God. It ought to appear in the same proportion to you. That which appears impossible to you is easy for God. Remember: *"... All things are possible to him who be-*

lieves." (Mark 9:23) Approach prayer with anticipation, not doubt. Unless you pray in the mind and nature of Jesus Christ, your prayer will be like an arrow shot into the air, without course and without target. An aimless prayer verges on futility. But do not wait until you believe your mind is at the level of Jesus Christ's. The act of praying in faith lifts your consciousness toward His. "And in praying use not vain repetitions" but let your words come new from your heart. Practice prayer until your mind is cleansed and your words are formed in love and faith so they may be acceptable in His sight.

Now I hope I haven't made it seem too difficult.

Some appear to pray only when disaster is imminent. That, they say, is when they need help; at other times they can pretty well take care of things by themselves. There is no condemnation in the love of God; He helps you whenever you call, as few or as many times as you choose. He helps you always. Whether or not you call, you do not shut Him out. But for your own good you need to pray consistently. You need to maintain a prayerful attitude. Besides, we all need the practice.

Let us praise and give thanks to God that

He never says no to our prayers. He answers every kind of prayer, casual, pleading, wheedling, demanding, frightened, or no prayer at all, just so long as we open our minds to let Him in. He is ever picking us up when we fall, steadying us when we stumble, propping us up when we weaken.

We can make it easier for Him and for ourselves by seeing ourselves in the same image as He sees us. He sees us as perfect, His creation of perfection without flaw. Many of us see ourselves as being a long way from perfection. This is all right to a point, because it reminds us that we need to improve. But when it takes us down so far that we see no way back to His ideal, we have set a stumbling block in our path. Let us set about changing things quickly. Make a practice of seeing yourself without fault, and acting as you will when it is true. If you continue in this vein, your mind will at last insist that you become in fact perfect. One by one your old faults and weaknesses and failings will relinquish their hold on you and shuffle off into the mists of what used to be.

We are creatures of upward action. We have a built-in demand to work for improvement in ourselves. We attain a goal and immediately desire a higher one. We are achieving organisms with a necessity to achieve, making ourselves miserable when we seem to fail to achieve, or to move too slowly.

The moving spirit of God motivates us from the day we are born until the day we die, and we cannot be truly happy unless we have a sense of fulfillment. Fulfillment comes from knowing that we have gained, or are on the way to gaining, the manifestation of the deep and fruitful and good desires of our hearts. Fulfillment is ours through prayer which lifts our consciousness into at-one-ment with God and Principle and divine law. This is what prayer does for us. It is by the grace of God a privilege and ineffable joy.

Thank God for prayer!

Russell Lake has been a Truth student since the 1940s and has been writing for Unity publications most of that time. Although this is his first book for Unity, he has written scores of articles. He and his wife, Cecil, live in Fresno, California. Cecil is an ordained Unity minister and has served congregations in Merced and Fresno. Russell has assisted her through the years.

After retirement from his advertising business, Russell and Cecil lived out a lifelong dream—a three-month trip, covering 2,000 miles, by boat on the Yukon River in Alaska.

Printed U.S.A.
165-F-6425-15M-11-83